MW01092368

Kali Linux Wireless Penetration Testing Beginner's Guide

Third Edition

Master wireless testing techniques to survey and attack wireless networks with Kali Linux, including the KRACK attack

Cameron Buchanan

Vivek Ramachandran

BIRMINGHAM - MUMBAI

Kali Linux Wireless Penetration Testing Beginner's Guide
Third Edition

First published: September 2011

Second edition: March 2015

Third edition: December 2017

Production reference: 1261217

Published by Packt Publishing Ltd.
Livery Place
35 Livery Street
Birmingham B3 2PB, UK.

ISBN 978-1-78883-192-5

www.packtpub.com

Credits

Authors
Cameron Buchanan
Vivek Ramachandran

Reviewer
Daniel W. Dieterle

Acquisition Editor
Ben Renow-Clarke

Project Editor
Suzanne Coutinho

Technical Editor
Bhagyashree Rai

Proofreader
Safis Editing

Indexer
Rekha Nair

Graphics
Tom Scaria

Production Coordinator
Arvindkumar Gupta

Disclaimer

The content within this book is for educational purposes only. It is designed to help users test their own system against information security threats and protect their IT infrastructure from similar attacks. Packt Publishing and the authors of this book take no responsibility for actions resulting from the inappropriate usage of learning material contained within this book.

About the Authors

Cameron Buchanan is a penetration tester by trade and a writer in his spare time. He has performed penetration tests around the world for a variety of clients across many industries. Previously, Cameron was a member of the RAF. In his spare time, he enjoys doing stupid things, such as trying to make things fly, getting electrocuted, and dunking himself in freezing cold water. He is married and lives in London.

Vivek Ramachandran has been working on Wi-Fi security since 2003. He discovered the Caffe Latte attack and also broke WEP Cloaking, a WEP protection schema, publicly in 2007 at DEF CON. In 2011, he was the first to demonstrate how malware could use Wi-Fi to create backdoors, worms, and even botnets.

Earlier, Vivek was one of the programmers of the 802.1x protocol and Port Security in Cisco's 6500 Catalyst series of switches, and he was also one of the winners of the Microsoft Security Shootout contest held in India among a reported 65,000 participants. He is best known in the hacker community as the founder of SecurityTube.net, where he routinely posts videos on Wi-Fi security, assembly language, exploitation techniques, and so on. SecurityTube.net receives over 100,000 unique visitors a month.

Vivek's work on wireless security has been quoted in BBC Online, InfoWorld, MacWorld, The Register, IT World Canada, and so on. This year, he will speak or train at a number of security conferences, including Blackhat, DEF CON, Hacktivity, 44con, HITB-ML, BruCON Derbycon, Hashdays, SecurityZone, and SecurityByte.

About the Reviewer

Daniel W. Dieterle is an internationally published security author, researcher, and technical editor. He has over 20 years of IT experience and has provided various levels of support and service to hundreds of companies, ranging from small businesses to large corporations. Daniel authors and runs the Cyber Arms - Security Blog (`https://cyberarms.wordpress.com/`) and an Internet of Things projects and security-based blog (`https://dantheiotman.com/`).

www.PacktPub.com

eBooks, discount offers, and more

Did you know that Packt offers eBook versions of every book published, with PDF and ePub files available? You can upgrade to the eBook version at www.PacktPub.com and as a print book customer, you are entitled to a discount on the eBook copy. Get in touch with us at customercare@packtpub.com for more details.

At www.PacktPub.com, you can also read a collection of free technical articles, sign up for a range of free newsletters and receive exclusive discounts and offers on Packt books and eBooks.

https://www.packtpub.com/mapt

Get the most in-demand software skills with Mapt. Mapt gives you full access to all Packt books and video courses, as well as industry-leading tools to help you plan your personal development and advance your career.

Why subscribe?

- ◆ Fully searchable across every book published by Packt
- ◆ Copy and paste, print, and bookmark content
- ◆ On demand and accessible via a web browser

Customer Feedback

Thanks for purchasing this Packt book. At Packt, quality is at the heart of our editorial process. To help us improve, please leave us an honest review on this book's Amazon page at `https://www.amazon.com/dp/1788831926`.

If you'd like to join our team of regular reviewers, you can email us at `customerreviews@packtpub.com`. We award our regular reviewers with free eBooks and videos in exchange for their valuable feedback. Help us be relentless in improving our products!

Table of Contents

Preface

Wireless networks have become ubiquitous in today's world. Millions of people use it worldwide every day at their homes, offices, and public hotspots to log on to the internet and do both personal and professional work. Even though wireless makes life incredibly easy and gives us such great mobility, it comes with its risks. In recent times, insecure wireless networks have been used to break into companies, banks, and government organizations. The frequency of these attacks is only intensified, as network administrators are still clueless on how to secure wireless networks in a robust and fool proof way.

Kali Linux Wireless Penetration Testing Beginner's Guide, *Third Edition*, is aimed at helping the reader understand the insecurities associated with wireless networks, and how to conduct penetration tests to find and plug them. This is an essential read for those who would like to conduct security audits on wireless networks and always wanted a step-by-step practical guide for this. With this book, your learning will be complete, as every wireless attack explained is immediately followed by a practical demo.

We have chosen Kali Linux as the platform to test all the wireless attacks in this book. Kali Linux, as you might already be aware, is the world's most popular penetration testing distribution. It contains hundreds of security and hacking tools, some of which we will use in this book.

What this book covers

Chapter 1, *Wireless Lab Setup*, shows how to create a wireless testing lab using off-the-shelf hardware and open source software. In order to be able to try out the dozens of exercises in this book, you will need to set up a wireless lab. We will first look at the hardware requirements, which include wireless cards, antennas, access points, and other Wi-Fi enabled devices. Then we will shift our focus to the software requirements, which include the operating system, Wi-Fi drivers, and security tools. Finally, we will create a test bed for our experiments and verify the different wireless configurations on it.

Chapter 2, WLAN and Its Inherent Insecurities, focuses on inherent design flaws in wireless networks that make insecure out of the box. We will begin with a quick recap of the 802.11 WLAN protocols using a network analyzer called Wireshark. This will give us a practical understanding about how these protocols work. Most importantly, we will see how client and access point communication work at the packer level by analyzing management, control, and data frames. We will then learn about packet injection and packer sniffing in wireless networks, and look at some tools that enable us to do this.

Chapter 3, Bypassing WLAN Authentication, reveals how you can break WLAN authentication mechanism! We will go step by step, and explore how to subvert Open Authentication and Shared Key Authentication. While doing this, you will learn how to analyze wireless packets and figure out the authentication mechanism of the network. We will also look at how to break into networks with Hidden SSID and MAC Filtering enabled. These are two common mechanisms employed by network administrators to make wireless networks more stealthy and difficult to penetrate, however, these are extremely simple to bypass.

Chapter 4, WLAN Encryption Flaws, describes one of the most vulnerable parts of the WLAN protocol, which is the encryption schemas—WEP, WPA, and WPA2. Over the past decade, hackers have found multiple flaws in these schemas and have written publically available software to break them and decrypt the data. Also, even though WPA/WPA2 are secure by design, misconfiguring these opens up security vulnerabilities, which can be easily exploited. In this chapter, you will understand the insecurities in each of these encryption schemas, and you'll perform practical demos on how to break them.

Chapter 5, Attacks on the WLAN Infrastructure, shifts your focus to WLAN infrastructure vulnerabilities. We will look at vulnerabilities created due to both configuration and design problems. We will also do practical demos of attacks, namely access point MAC spoofing, bit flipping and replay attacks, rogue access points, fuzzing, and denial of service. This chapter will you a solid understanding of how to do a penetration test of the WLAN infrastructure.

Chapter 6, Attacking the Client, might open your eyes if you always believed that wireless client security was something you did not have to worry about! Most people exclude the client from their list when they think about WLAN security. This chapter will prove beyond doubt why the client is just as important as the access point when penetration testing a WLAN network. We will look at how to compromise the security using client-side attacks such as misassociation, Caffe Latte, disassociation, ad-hoc connections, fuzzing, and honeypots.

Chapter 7, Advanced WLAN Attacks, looks at more advanced attacks, now that we have already covered most of the basic attacks on both the infrastructure and the client. These attacks typically involve using multiple basic attacks in conjunction to break security in more challenging scenarios. Some of these attacks include wireless device fingerprinting, man-in-the-middle over wireless, evading wireless intrusion detection and prevention systems, and rogue access point operating using custom protocol. This chapter presents the absolute bleeding edge in wireless attacks out in the real world.

Chapter 8, KRACK Attacks, investigates the new set of vulnerabilities discovered in 2017, regarding the WPA2 handshake. Your knowledge of the WPA2 handshake is refreshed and examined in detail to see how these new attacks apply.

Chapter 9, Attacking WPA-Enterprise and RADIUS, graduates you to the next level by introducing advanced attacks on WPA-Enterprise and the RADIUS server set up. These attacks will come in handy when you have to penetration test large enterprise networks that rely on WPA-Enterprise and RADIUS authentication to provide them with security.

Chapter 10, WLAN Penetration Testing Methodology, is where all the learning from the previous chapters comes together, and we will look at how to do a wireless penetration test in a systematic and methodical way. You will learn about the various phases of penetrating testing—Planning, Discovery, Attack, and Reporting, and apply it to wireless penetration testing. We will also understand how to propose recommendations and best practices after a wireless penetration test.

Chapter 11, WPS and Probes, covers the two new attacks in the industry that have developed since the initial publication—WPS brute-force and probe sniffing for monitoring.

What you need for this book

To follow and recreate the practical exercises in this book, you will need two laptops with built in Wi-Fi cards, a USB wireless Wi-Fi adapter, Kali Linux, and some other hardware and software. We have detailed this in *Chapter 1, Wireless Lab Setup*.

As an alternative to the two laptop setup, you can also create a virtual machine housing Kali Linux and connect the card to it using the USB interface. This will help you get started with using this book much faster, but we would recommend that you use a dedicated machine running Kali Linux for actual assessments in the field.

From a prerequisite perspective, you should be aware of the basics of wireless networks. This includes having prior knowledge about the basics of the 802.11 protocol and client-access point communication. Though we will briefly touch upon some of this when we set up the lab, it is expected that you are already aware of these concepts.

Who this book is for

Though this book is a Beginner's series, it is meant for all levels of users, from amateurs to wireless security experts. There is something for everyone. The book starts with simple attacks and then moves on to explain the more complicated ones, and finally, discusses bleeding edge attacks and research. As all attacks are explained using practical demonstrations, it is very easy for readers at all levels to quickly try out the attacks by themselves. Please note that even though the book highlights the different attacks that can be launched against a wireless network, the real purpose is to educate the user to become a wireless penetration tester. An adept penetration tester will understand all the attacks here and will be able to demonstrate them with ease, if requested by his client.

Sections

In this book, you will find several headings that appear frequently (*Time for action*, *What just happened?*, *Pop quiz*, and *Have a go hero*).

To give clear instructions on how to complete a procedure or task, we use these sections as follows:

Time for action – heading

1. Action 1
2. Action 2
3. Action 3

Instructions often need some extra explanation to ensure that they make sense, so they are followed with these sections:

What just happened?

This section explains the working of the tasks or instructions that you have just completed.

You will also find some other learning aids in the book, for example:

Pop quiz – heading

These are short multiple-choice questions intended to help you test your own understanding.

Have a go hero – heading

These are practical challenges that give you ideas to experiment with what you have learned.

Conventions

You will also find a number of text styles that distinguish between different kinds of information. Here are some examples of these styles and an explanation of their meaning.

Code words in text, database table names, folder names, filenames, file extensions, pathnames, dummy URLs, user input, and Twitter handles are shown as follows: "Plug in the card to one of the Kali laptop's USB ports and boot it. Once you log in, open a console terminal and type in `iwconfig`."

A block of code is set as follows:

```
import subprocess
import datetime
results = open("results.txt", "a")
while 1:
    cmd = subprocess.check_output(["tshark -n -i wlan0mon -T fields -e
wlan.sa -e wlan.ssid -c 100"], shell=True)
    split = cmd.split("\n")
    for value in split[:-1]:
        if value.strip():
                splitvalue = value.split("\t")
                MAC = str(splitvalue[0])
                SSID = str(splitvalue[1])
                time = str(datetime.datetime.now())
                results.write(MAC+" "+SSID+" "+time+"\r\n")
```

When we wish to draw your attention to a particular part of a code block, the relevant lines or items are set in bold:

```
import subprocess
import datetime
results = open("results.txt", "a")
while 1:
    cmd = subprocess.check_output(["tshark -n -i wlan0mon -T fields -e
wlan.sa -e wlan.ssid -c 100"], shell=True)
    split = cmd.split("\n")
    for value in split[:-1]:
            if value.strip():
```

```
splitvalue = value.split("\t")
MAC = str(splitvalue[0])
SSID = str(splitvalue[1])
time = str(datetime.datetime.now())
results.write(MAC+" "+SSID+" "+time+"\r\n")
```

Any command-line input or output is written as follows:

```
ifconfig wlan0 up
```

New terms and **important words** are shown in bold. Words that you see on the screen, in menus, or dialog boxes, for example, appear in the text like this: "Boot the laptop with this DVD and select the **Install** from **Boot menu** option."

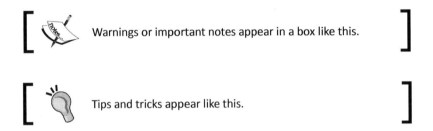

Warnings or important notes appear in a box like this.

Tips and tricks appear like this.

Reader feedback

Feedback from our readers is always welcome. Let us know what you think about this book—what you liked or disliked. Reader feedback is important for us as it helps us develop titles that you will really get the most out of.

To send us general feedback, simply email feedback@packtpub.com, and mention the book's title in the subject of your message.

If there is a topic that you have expertise in and you are interested in either writing or contributing to a book, see our author guide at www.packtpub.com/authors.

Customer support

Now that you are the proud owner of a Packt book, we have a number of things to help you to get the most from your purchase.

Downloading the example code

You can download the example code files for this book from your account at `http://www.packtpub.com`. If you purchased this book elsewhere, you can visit `http://www.packtpub.com/support` and register to have the files e-mailed directly to you.

You can download the code files by following these steps:

1. Log in or register to our website using your e-mail address and password.
2. Hover the mouse pointer on the **SUPPORT** tab at the top.
3. Click on **Code Downloads & Errata**.
4. Enter the name of the book in the **Search** box.
5. Select the book for which you're looking to download the code files.
6. Choose from the drop-down menu where you purchased this book from.
7. Click on **Code Download**.

You can also download the code files by clicking on the **Code Files** button on the book's webpage at the Packt Publishing website. This page can be accessed by entering the book's name in the **Search** box. Please note that you need to be logged in to your Packt account.

Once the file is downloaded, please make sure that you unzip or extract the folder using the latest version of:

◆ WinRAR / 7-Zip for Windows
◆ Zipeg / iZip / UnRarX for Mac
◆ 7-Zip / PeaZip for Linux

The code bundle for the book is also hosted on GitHub at `https://github.com/PacktPublishing/Kali-Linux-Wireless-Penetration-Testing-Beginners-Guide-Third-Edition`. We also have other code bundles from our rich catalog of books and videos available at `https://github.com/PacktPublishing/`. Check them out!

Downloading the color images of this book

We also provide you with a PDF file that has color images of the screenshots/ diagrams used in this book. The color images will help you better understand the changes in the output. You can download this file from `https://www.packtpub.com/sites/default/files/downloads/KaliLinuxWirelessPenetrationTestingBeginnersGuideThirdEdition_ColorImages.pdf`.

Errata

Although we have taken every care to ensure the accuracy of our content, mistakes do happen. If you find a mistake in one of our books—maybe a mistake in the text or the code—we would be grateful if you could report this to us. By doing so, you can save other readers from frustration and help us improve subsequent versions of this book. If you find any errata, please report them by visiting http://www.packtpub.com/submit-errata, selecting your book, clicking on the **Errata Submission Form** link, and entering the details of your errata. Once your errata are verified, your submission will be accepted and the errata will be uploaded to our website or added to any list of existing errata under the Errata section of that title.

To view the previously submitted errata, go to https://www.packtpub.com/books/content/support and enter the name of the book in the search field. The required information will appear under the **Errata** section.

Piracy

Piracy of copyrighted material on the internet is an ongoing problem across all media. At Packt, we take the protection of our copyright and licenses very seriously. If you come across any illegal copies of our works in any form on the internet, please provide us with the location address or website name immediately so that we can pursue a remedy.

Please contact us at copyright@packtpub.com with a link to the suspected pirated material.

We appreciate your help in protecting our authors and our ability to bring you valuable content.

Questions

If you have a problem with any aspect of this book, you can contact us at questions@packtpub.com, and we will do our best to address the problem.

1
Wireless Lab Setup

"If I had eight hours to chop down a tree, I'd spend six hours sharpening my axe."

— Abraham Lincoln, 16th US President

Behind every successful execution is hours or days of preparation, and wireless penetration testing is no exception. In this chapter, we will create a wireless lab that we will use for our experiments in this book. Consider this lab as your preparation arena before you dive into real-world penetration testing!

Wireless penetration testing is a practical subject, and it is important to first set up a lab, where we can try out all the different experiments in this book in a safe and controlled environment. It is important that you set up this lab first before moving on in this book.

In this chapter, we will take a look at the following:

- Hardware and software requirements
- Installing Kali
- Setting up an access point and configuring it
- Installing the wireless card
- Testing connectivity between the laptop and the access point

So let the games begin!

Hardware requirements

We will need the following hardware to set up the wireless lab:

- **Two laptops with internal Wi-Fi cards**: We will use one of the laptops as the victim in our lab and the other as the penetration tester's laptop. Though almost any laptop would fit this profile, laptops with at least 3 GB RAM are desirable. This is because we may be running a lot of memory-intensive software in our experiments.

- **One wireless adapter (optional)**: Depending on the wireless card of your laptop, we may need a USB Wi-Fi card that can support packet injection and packet sniffing, which is supported by Kali. The best choice seems to be the Alfa AWUS036H card from Alfa Networks, as Kali supports this out of the box. This is available on www.amazon.com for a retail price of £18 at the time of writing. An alternative option is the Edimax EW-7711UAN, which is smaller and, marginally, cheaper.

- **One access point**: Any access8 point that supports WEP/WPA/WPA2 encryption standards would fit the bill. I will be using a TP-LINK TL-WR841N Wireless router for the purpose of illustration in this book. You can purchase it from www.amazon.com for a retail price of around £20 at the time of writing.

- **An internet connection**: This will come in handy for performing research, downloading software, and for some of our experiments.

Software requirements

We will need the following software to set up the wireless lab:

- **Kali**: This software can be downloaded from the official website located at http://www.kali.org. The software is open source, and you should be able to download it directly from the website.

- **Windows XP/Vista/7/10**: You will need any one of Windows XP, Windows Vista, Windows 7, or Windows 10 installed on one of the laptops. This laptop will be used as the victim machine for the rest of the book.

 Important to note is that even though we are using a Windows-based OS for our tests, the techniques learnt can be applied to any Wi-Fi-capable devices, such as smartphones and tablets, among others.

Installing Kali

Let's now quickly take a look at how to get up and running with Kali.

Kali will be installed on the laptop that will serve as the penetration tester's machine for the rest of the book.

Time for action – installing Kali

Kali is relatively simple to install. We will run Kali by booting it as a live DVD, and then install it on the hard drive.

Perform the following instructions step by step:

1. Burn the Kali ISO (we are using the Kali 32-bit ISO) you downloaded, onto a bootable DVD.

2. Boot the laptop with this DVD and select the option **Install** from **Boot menu**:

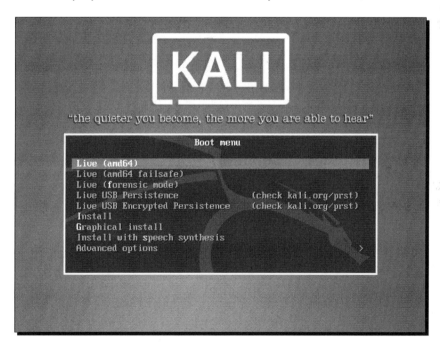

3. If booting was successful, then you should see an awesome retro screen as shown in the following screenshot:

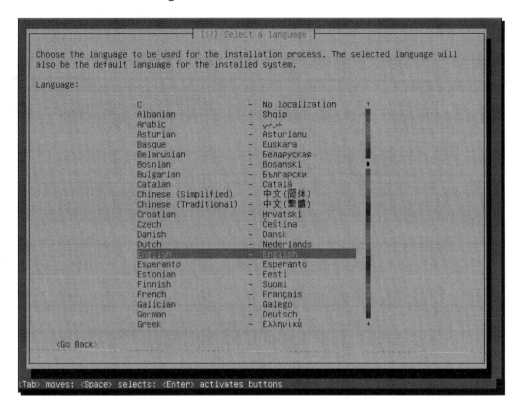

4. This installer is similar to the GUI-based installers of most Linux systems and should be simple to follow. Select the appropriate options on every screen and start the installation process. Once the installation is done, restart the machine as prompted and remove the DVD.

5. Once the machine restarts, a login screen will be displayed. Log in as `root` and the password is whatever you set it to during the installation process. You should now be logged into your installed version of Kali. Congratulations!

6. I will change the desktop theme and some settings for this book. Feel free to use your own themes and color settings!

What just happened?

We have successfully installed Kali on the laptop! We will use this laptop as the penetration tester's laptop for all other experiments in this book.

Have a go hero – installing Kali on VirtualBox

We can also install Kali within virtualization software such as VirtualBox. If you don't want to dedicate a full laptop to Kali, this is the best option. Kali's installation process in VirtualBox is exactly the same. The only difference is the pre-setup, which you will have to create in VirtualBox. Have a go at it! You can download VirtualBox from `http://www.virtualbox.org`.

One of the other ways in which we can install and use Kali is via USB drives. This is particularly useful if you do not want to install on the hard drive, but still want to store persistent data, such as scripts and new tools, on your Kali instance. We encourage you to try this out as well!

Setting up the access point

Now we will set up the access point. As mentioned earlier, we will be using the TP-LINK TL-WR841N Wireless router for all the experiments in this book. However, feel free to use any other access point. The basic principles of operation and usage remain the same.

Time for action – configuring the access point

Let's begin! We will set the access point up to use **Open Authentication (OAuth)** with an SSID of `Wireless Lab`.

Follow these instructions step by step:

1. Power on the access point, and use an Ethernet cable to connect your laptop to one of the access point's Ethernet ports.

2. Enter the IP address of the access point configuration terminal in your browser. For TP-Link, it is by default `192.168.1.1`. You should consult your access point's setup guide to find its IP address. If you do not have the manuals for the access point, you can also find the IP address by running the `route -n` command. The gateway IP address is typically the access point's IP. Once you are connected, you should see a configuration portal that looks like the following **TP-LINK Wireless N Router WR841N** emblazoned screenshot:

3. Explore the various settings in the portal after logging in, and find the settings related to configuring a new SSID.

4. Change the SSID to `Wireless Lab`. Depending on the access point, you may have to reboot it for the settings to change.

5. Similarly, find the settings related to **Wireless Security** and change the setting to **Disable Security**. **Disable Security** indicates that it is using the Open Authentication mode.

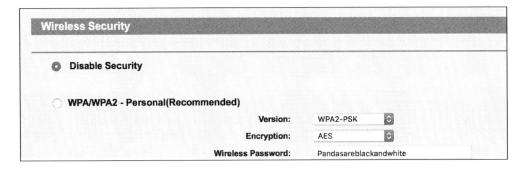

6. Save the changes to the access point and reboot it, if required. Now your access point should be up-and-running with an SSID, `Wireless Lab`.

An easy way to verify this is to use the wireless configuration utility in Windows and observe the available networks using the Windows laptop. You should find `Wireless Lab` as one of the networks in the listing:

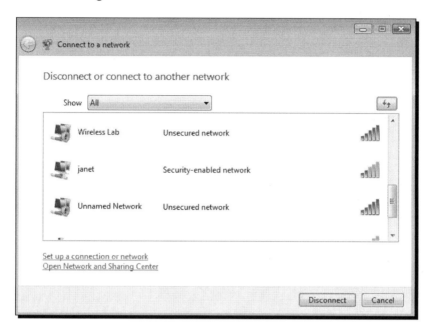

What just happened?

We have successfully set up our access point with an SSID, `Wireless Lab`. It is broadcasting its presence, and this is being picked up by our Windows laptop and others within the **Radio Frequency (RF)** range of the access point.

Important to note is that we configured our access point in the **Open** mode, which is the least secure. It is advisable not to connect this access point to the internet for the time being, as anyone within the RF range will be able to use it to access the internet.

Have a go hero – configuring the access point to use WEP and WPA

Play around with the configuration options of your access point. Try to get it up-and-running using encryption schemes such as WEP and WPA/WPA2. We will use these modes in later chapters to illustrate attacks against them.

Setting up the wireless card

Setting up our wireless adapter is much easier than the access point. The advantage is that Kali supports this card out of the box and ships with all requisite device drivers to enable packet injection and packet sniffing.

Time for action – configuring your wireless card

We will be using the wireless adapter with the penetration tester's laptop.

Follow these instructions step by step to set up your card:

1. Plug in the card to one of the Kali laptop's USB ports and boot it. Once you log in, open a console terminal and type in `iwconfig`. Your screen should look as follows:

```
                        root@wireless-example: ~

  File  Edit  View  Search  Terminal  Help
root@wireless-example:~# iwconfig
wlan0     IEEE 802.11bgn  ESSID:off/any
          Mode:Managed  Access Point: Not-Associated    Tx-Power=20 dBm
          Retry short limit:7   RTS thr:off   Fragment thr:off
          Encryption key:off
          Power Management:off

lo        no wireless extensions.

eth0      no wireless extensions.
```

As you can see, `wlan0` is the wireless interface created for the wireless adapter.

Type in `ifconfig wlan0 up` to bring the interface up. Then, type in `ifconfig wlan0` to see the current state of the interface:

```
root@wireless-example:~# ifconfig wlan0
wlan0     Link encap:Ethernet  HWaddr 80:1f:02:8f:34:d5
          UP BROADCAST MULTICAST  MTU:1500  Metric:1
          RX packets:0 errors:0 dropped:0 overruns:0 frame:0
          TX packets:0 errors:0 dropped:0 overruns:0 carrier:0
          collisions:0 txqueuelen:1000
          RX bytes:0 (0.0 B)  TX bytes:0 (0.0 B)
```

2. The MAC address `00:c0:ca:3e:bd:93` should look like the MAC address written under your Alfa card. I am using the Edimax that gives me the preceding MAC address `80:1f:02:8f:34:d5`. This is a quick check to ensure that you have enabled the correct interface.

What just happened?

Kali ships with all the required drivers for the Alfa and Edimax adapters out of the box. As soon as the machine booted, the adapter was recognized and was assigned the network interface `wlan0`. Now our wireless adapter is up and functional!

Connecting to the access point

Now we will take a look at how to connect to the access point using the wireless adapter. Our access point has an SSID, `Wireless Lab` and does not use any authentication.

Time for action – configuring your wireless card

Here we go! Follow these steps to connect your wireless card to the access point:

1. Let's first see what wireless networks our adapter is currently detecting. Issue the `iwlist wlan0 scanning` command, and you will find a list of networks in your vicinity:

```
root@wireless-example:~# iwlist wlan0 scanning
wlan0     Scan completed :
          Cell 01 - Address: 9C:D3:6D:2A:7B:C0
                    Channel:11
                    Frequency:2.462 GHz (Channel 11)
                    Quality=22/70  Signal level=-88 dBm
                    Encryption key:on
                    ESSID:"everythingwillprobablynotbeokay"
                    Bit Rates:1 Mb/s; 2 Mb/s; 5.5 Mb/s; 11 Mb/s; 6 Mb/s
                              9 Mb/s; 12 Mb/s; 18 Mb/s
                    Bit Rates:24 Mb/s; 36 Mb/s; 48 Mb/s; 54 Mb/s
                    Mode:Master
                    Extra:tsf=0000023369666b3c
                    Extra: Last beacon: 1172ms ago
                    IE: Unknown: 001F65766572797468696E6777696C6C70726F6261626C79
96E6F7462656F6B6179
                    IE: Unknown: 010882848B960C121824
                    IE: Unknown: 03010B
                    IE: Unknown: 0706474220010D14
                    IE: Unknown: 2A0104
                    IE: Unknown: 32043048606C
                    IE: Unknown: 2D1AAD011BFFFF000000000000000000000000000000000040
6E6E70D00
```

Keep scrolling down and you should find the `Wireless Lab` network in this list. In my setup, it is detected as `Cell 05`; it may be different in yours. The `ESSID` field contains the network name.

2. As multiple access points can have the same SSID, verify that the MAC address mentioned in the preceding `Address` field matches your access point's MAC. A fast and easy way to get the MAC address is underneath the access point or using web-based GUI settings.

3. Now, issue the `iwconfig wlan0 essid "Wireless Lab"` command and then `iwconfig wlan0` to check the status. If you have successfully connected to the access point, you should see the MAC address of the access point in the `Access Point` field in the output of `iwconfig`.

4. We know that the access point has a management interface IP address `192.168.0.1` from its manual. Alternately, this is the same as the default router IP address when we run the `route -n` command. Let's set our IP address in the same subnet by issuing the `ifconfig wlan0 192.168.0.2 netmask 255.255.255.0 up` command. Verify that the command succeeded by typing `ifconfig wlan0` and checking the output.

5. Now let's ping the access point by issuing the `ping 192.168.0.1` command. If the network connection has been set up properly, then you should see the responses from the access point. You can additionally issue an `arp -a` command to verify that the response is coming from the access point. You should see that the MAC address of the IP `192.168.0.1` is the access point's MAC address we noted earlier. It is important to note that some of the more recent access points might have responses to the **Internet Control Message Protocol (ICMP)** echo request packets disabled. This is typically done to make the access point secure out of the box with only minimal configuration settings available. In such a case, you can try to launch a browser and access the web interface to verify that the connection is up-and-running:

```
root@wireless-example:~# ping 192.168.0.1
PING 192.168.0.1 (192.168.0.1) 56(84) bytes of data.
64 bytes from 192.168.0.1: icmp_req=1 ttl=128 time=5.02 ms
64 bytes from 192.168.0.1: icmp_req=2 ttl=128 time=1.48 ms
64 bytes from 192.168.0.1: icmp_req=3 ttl=128 time=1.47 ms
^C
--- 192.168.0.1 ping statistics ---
3 packets transmitted, 3 received, 0% packet loss, time 2003ms
rtt min/avg/max/mdev = 1.479/2.660/5.021/1.670 ms
```

6. On the access point, we can verify connectivity by looking at the connection logs. As you can see in the following log, the MAC address of the wireless card 4C:0F:6E:70:BD:CB has been logged making DHCP requests from the router:

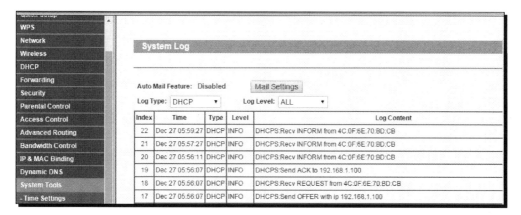

What just happened?

We just connected to our access point successfully from Kali using our wireless adapter as the wireless device. We also learned how to verify that a connection has been established at both the wireless client and the access point side.

Have a go hero – establishing a connection in a WEP configuration

Here is a challenging exercise for you: set up the access point in a WEP configuration. For each of these, try establishing a connection with the access point using the wireless adapter. Hint: check the manual for the iwconfig command by typing man iwconfig to see how to configure the card to connect to WEP.

Pop quiz – understanding the basics

Q1. After issuing the ifconfig wlan0 command, how do you verify that the wireless card is up and functional?

Q2. Can we run all our experiments using the Kali live CD alone? Can we not install the CD to the hard drive?

Q3. What does the arp -a command show?

Q4. Which tool should we use in Kali to connect to WPA/WPA2 networks?

Summary

This chapter provided you with detailed instructions on how to set up your own wireless lab. Also, in the process, you learned the basic steps do the following:

- ◆ Installing Kali on your hard drive and exploring other options such as virtual machines and USBs
- ◆ Configuring your access point over the web interface
- ◆ Understanding and using several commands to configure and use your wireless card
- ◆ Verifying the connection state between the wireless client and the access point

Gaining confidence in configuring the system is important for you. If you aren't confident, it is advisable that you repeat the preceding examples a couple of times. In later chapters, we will design more complicated scenarios.

In the next chapter, you will learn about inherent design-based insecurities in the WLANs design. We will use the network analyzer tool, Wireshark, to understand these concepts in a practical way.

2
WLAN and Its Inherent Insecurities

"The loftier the building, the deeper the foundation must be laid."

– Thomas Kempis

Nothing great can be built on a weak foundation, and in our context, nothing secure can be built on something that is inherently insecure.

WLANs, by design, have certain insecurities that are relatively easy to exploit, for example, by packet spoofing, packet injection, and sniffing (this could even happen from far away). We will explore these flaws in this chapter.

In this chapter, we shall look at the following:

- ◆ Revisiting WLAN frames
- ◆ Different frame types and subtypes
- ◆ Using Wireshark to sniff management, control, and data frames
- ◆ Sniffing data packets for a given wireless network
- ◆ Injecting packets into a given wireless network

. Let's get started!

Revisiting WLAN frames

As this book deals with the security aspects of wireless, we will assume that you already have a basic understanding of the protocol and the packet headers. If not, or if it's been some time since you worked on wireless, this would be a good time to revisit this topic again.

Let's now quickly review some basic concepts of WLANs that most of you may already be aware of. In WLANs, communication happens over frames. A frame would have the following header structure:

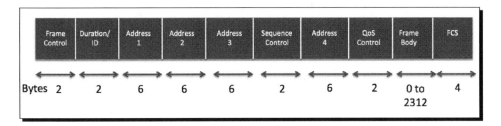

The Frame Control field itself has a more complex structure:

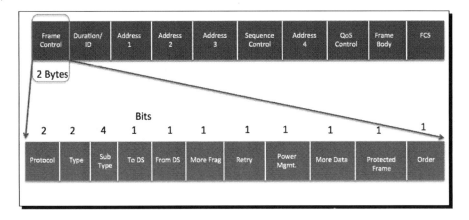

The `Type` field defines three types of WLAN frame:

- **Management frames**: Management frames are responsible for maintaining communication between access points and wireless clients. Management frames can have the following subtypes:
    - Authentication
    - Deauthentication
    - Association request
    - Association response
    - Reassociation request
    - Reassociation response
    - Disassociation
    - Beacon
    - Probe request
    - Probe response

- **Control frames**: Control frames are responsible for ensuring a proper exchange of data between access points and wireless clients. Control frames can have the following subtypes:
    - **Request to Send (RTS)**
    - **Clear to Send (CTS)**
    - **Acknowledgement (ACK)**

- **Data frames**: Data frames carry the actual data that is sent on the wireless network. There are no subtypes for data frames.

We will discuss the security implications of each of these frames when we discuss different attacks in later chapters.

We will now look at how to sniff these frames over a wireless network using Wireshark. There are other tools—such as Airodump-NG, Tcpdump, or Tshark—that you can use for sniffing as well. We will, however, mostly use Wireshark in this book, but we encourage you to explore other tools as well. The first step to do this is to create a monitor mode interface. This will create an interface for our adapter, which allows us to read all wireless frames in the air, regardless of whether they are destined for us or not. In the wired world, this is popularly called **promiscuous mode**.

Time for action – creating a monitor mode interface

Let's now set our wireless adapter to monitor mode.

Follow these instructions to get started:

1. Boot Kali with your adapter connected. Once you are within the console, enter `iwconfig` to confirm that your card has been detected and the driver has been loaded properly:

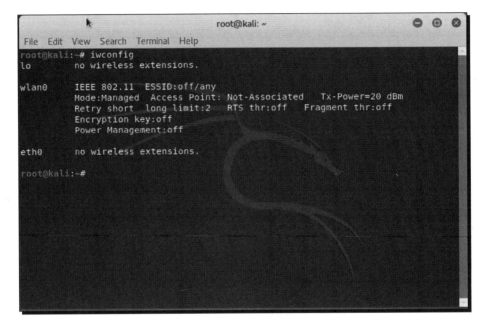

2. Use the `ifconfig wlan0 up` command to bring the card up (where `wlan0` is your adapter). Verify whether the card is up by running `ifconfig wlan0`. You should see the word UP in the first line of the output as shown in the following screenshot:

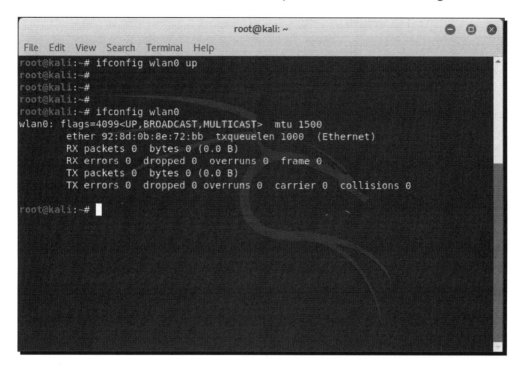

3. To put our card into monitor mode, we will use the `airmon-ng` utility that is available by default on Kali. First run the `airmon-ng` command to verify whether it detects the available cards. You should see the `wlan0` or `wlan1` interface listed in the output:

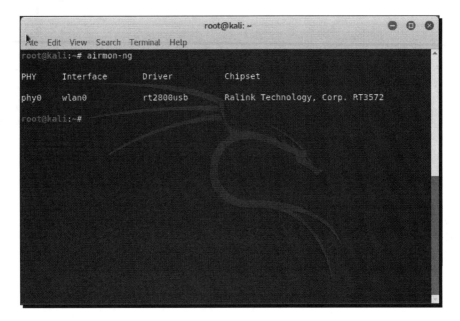

```
root@kali: ~
File  Edit  View  Search  Terminal  Help
root@kali:~# airmon-ng

PHY       Interface       Driver            Chipset

phy0      wlan0           rt2800usb         Ralink Technology, Corp. RT3572

root@kali:~#
```

4. Now enter the `airmon-ng start wlan0` command to create a monitor mode interface corresponding to the `wlan0` device. This new monitor mode interface will be named `wlan0mon`. (You can verify if it has been created by running `airmon-ng` without arguments again):

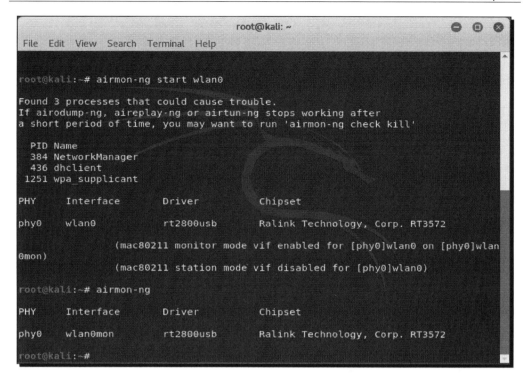

5. Also, running `ifconfig wlan0mon` should now display a new interface called `wlan0mon`:

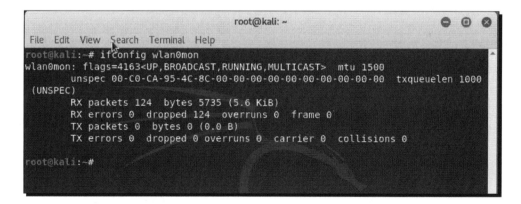

What just happened?

We have successfully created a monitor mode interface called `wlan0mon`. This interface will be used to sniff wireless packets off the air. This interface has been created for our wireless adapter.

Have a go hero – creating multiple monitor mode interfaces

It is possible to create multiple monitor mode interfaces using the same physical card. Use the `airmon-ng` utility to see how you can do this.

Awesome! We have a monitor mode interface just waiting to read some packets off the air. So let's get started.

In the next exercise, we will use Wireshark to sniff packets off the air using the `wlan0mon` monitor mode interface we just created.

Time for action – sniffing wireless packets

Follow the following instructions to begin sniffing packets:

1. Power up the access point `Wireless Lab` that we configured in *Chapter 1, Wireless Lab Setup*.

2. Start Wireshark by typing `Wireshark &` in the console. Once Wireshark is running, navigate to **Capture | Options**:

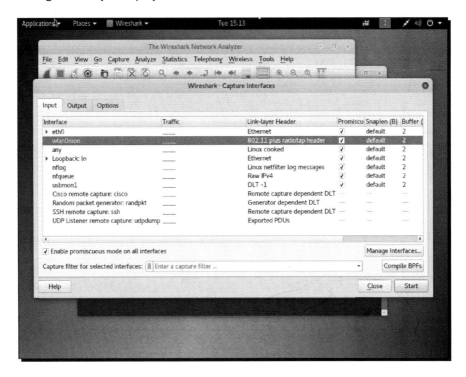

3. Select packet capture from the `wlan0mon` interface by clicking on the **Start** button at the bottom right of the interface as shown in the previous screenshot. Wireshark will begin the capture, and now you should see packets within the Wireshark window.

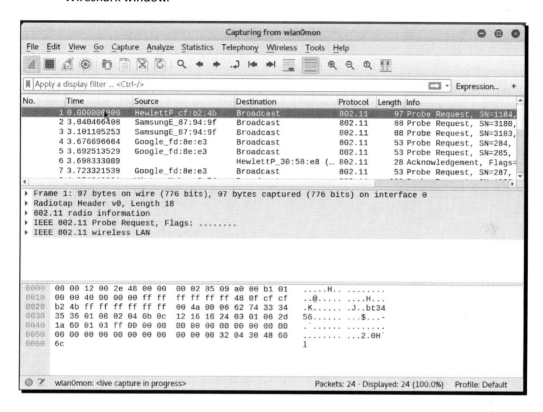

4. These are wireless packets that your wireless adapter is sniffing off the air. In order to view any packet, select it in the top window and the entire packet will be displayed in the middle window.

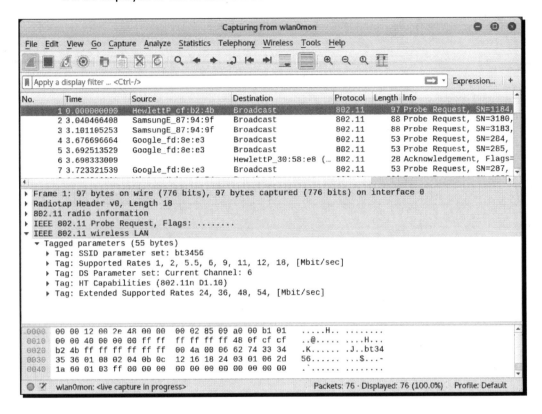

Click on the triangle in front of **IEEE 802.11 Wireless LAN** management frame to expand and view additional information.

Look at the different header fields in the packet and correlate them with the WLAN frame types and subtypes you learned earlier.

What just happened?

We just sniffed our first set of packets off the air! We launched Wireshark, which used the monitor mode interface, `wlan0mon` we created previously. You should notice, by looking at Wireshark's footer region, the speed at which the packets are being captured and also the number of packets captured till now.

Have a go hero – finding different devices

Wireshark traces can be a bit daunting at times; even for a reasonably populated wireless network, you could end up sniffing a few thousand packets. Hence, it is important to be able to drill down to those packets that interest us. This can be accomplished using filters in Wireshark. Explore how you can use these filters to identify unique wireless devices in the traces—both access points and wireless clients.

If you are unable to do this, don't worry as this is the next thing we will learn.

Time for action – viewing management, control, and data frames

Now we will learn how to apply filters in Wireshark to look at management, control, and data frames.

Please follow these instructions step by step:

1. To view all the management frames in the packets being captured, enter the filter `wlan.fc.type == 0` into the filter window and hit *Enter*. You can stop the packet capture if you want to prevent the packets from scrolling down too fast.

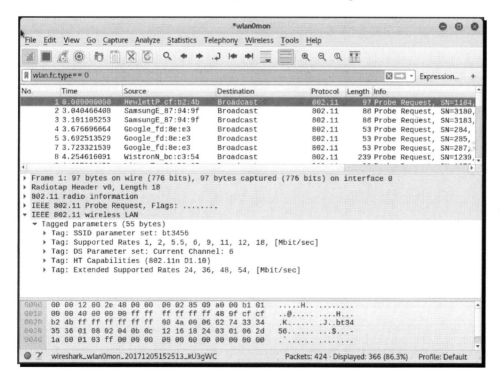

2. To view control frames, modify the filter expression to read `wlan.fc.type == 1`:

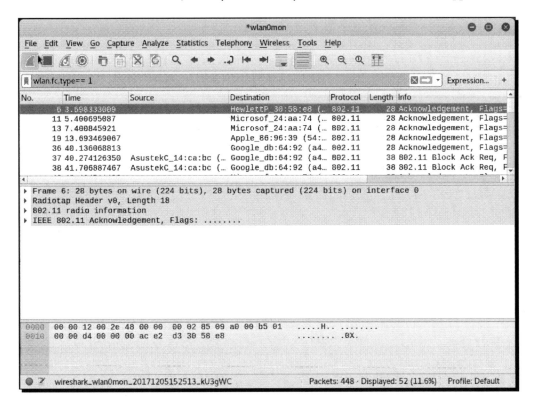

3. To view data frames, modify the filter expression to `wlan.fc.type == 2`:

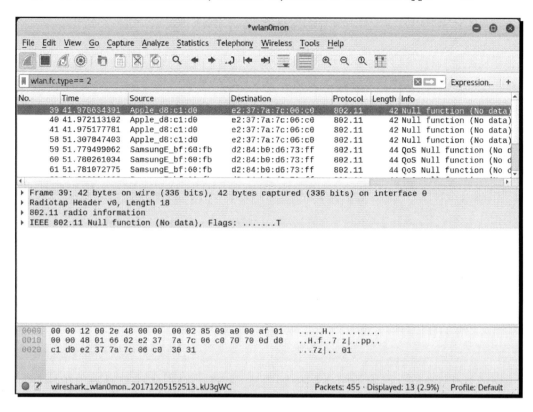

4. To additionally select a subtype, use the `wlan.fc.subtype` filter. For example, to view all the beacon frames among all management frames, use the following filter:

```
(wlan.fc.type == 0) && (wlan.fc.subtype == 8)
```

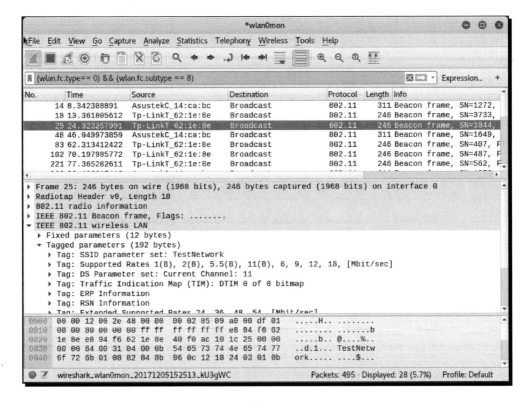

5. Alternatively, you can right-click on any of the header fields in the middle window and then select **Apply as Filter | Selected** to add it as a filter:

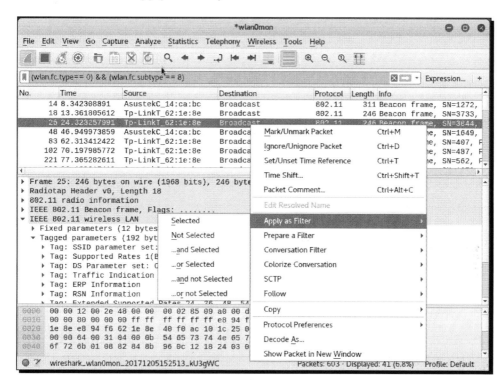

6. This will automatically add the correct filter expression for you in the **Filter** field.

What just happened?

We just learned how to filter packets in Wireshark using various filter expressions. This helps us monitor selected packets from devices we are interested in, instead of trying to analyze all the packets in the air.

Also, we can see that the packet headers of management, control, and data frames are in plain text and are not encrypted. Anyone who can sniff the packets can read these headers. It is also important to note that it is also possible for a hacker to modify any of these packets and retransmit them. As there is no integrity or replay attack mitigation in the protocol, this is very easy to do. We will look at some of these attacks in later chapters.

Have a go hero – playing with filters

You can consult Wireshark's manual to learn more about available filter expressions and how to use them. Try playing around with various filter combinations till you are confident that you can drill down to any level of detail, even in a very large packet trace.

In the next exercise, we will look at how to sniff data packets transferred between our access point and wireless client.

Time for action – sniffing data packets for our network

In this exercise, we will learn how to sniff data packets for a given wireless network. For the sake of simplicity, we will look at packets without any encryption.

Follow these instructions to get started:

1. Switch on the access point we named Wireless Lab. Let it remain configured to use no encryption.

2. We will first need to find the channel on which the Wireless Lab access point is running. To do this, open a terminal and run airodump-ng --bssid <mac> wlan0mon, where <mac> is the MAC address of our access point. Let the program run, and shortly you should see your access point shown on the screen along with the channel it is running on.

3. We can see from the preceding screenshot that our access point Wireless Lab is running on channel 11. Note that this may be different for your access point.

   In order to sniff data packets going to and from this access point, we need to lock our wireless card on the same channel, that is channel 11. To do this, run the iwconfig wlan0mon channel 11 command and then run iwconfig wlan0mon to verify it. You should see the Frequency: 2.462 GHz value in the output. This corresponds to channel 11.

```
                              root@kali: ~

 File  Edit  View  Search  Terminal  Help
root@kali:~# iwconfig wlan0mon channel 11
root@kali:~#
root@kali:~#
root@kali:~# iwconfig wlan0mon
wlan0mon  IEEE 802.11  Mode:Monitor  Frequency:2.462 GHz  Tx-Power=20 dBm
          Retry short  long limit:2  RTS thr:off  Fragment thr:off
          Power Management:off

root@kali:~#
```

4. Now fire up Wireshark and start sniffing on the `wlan0mon` interface. After Wireshark has started sniffing the packets, apply a filter for the `bssid` of our access point as shown in the following screenshot using `wlan.bssid == <mac>` in the filter area. Use the appropriate MAC address for your access point.

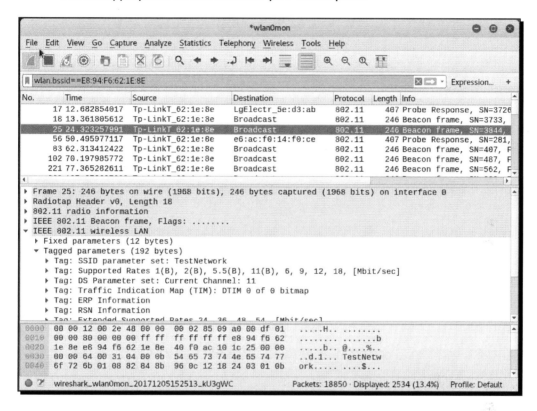

5. In order to see the data packets for our access point, add the following to the filter `(wlan.bssid == <mac>) && (wlan.fc.type_subtype == 0x20)`. Open your browser on the client laptop and type the URL of the access point in the management interface. In my case, as we have seen in *Chapter 1, Wireless Lab Setup*, it is `http://192.168.0.1`. This will generate data packets that Wireshark will capture.

6. Packet sniffing allows us to analyze unencrypted data packets very easily. This is the reason why we need to use encryption in wireless.

What just happened?

We have just sniffed data packets over the air with Wireshark using various filters. As our access point is not using any encryption, we are able to see all the data in plain text. This is a major security issue as anyone within RF range of the access point can see all the packets if he uses a sniffer such as Wireshark.

Have a go hero – analyzing data packets

Use Wireshark to analyze the data packets further. You will notice that a DHCP request is made by the client and, if a DHCP server is available, it responds with an address. Then you will find ARP packets and other protocol packets on the air. This is a nice and simple way to do passive host discovery on the wireless network. It is important to be able to see a packet trace and reconstruct how applications on the wireless host are communicating with the rest of the network. One of the interesting features Wireshark provides is the ability to follow a stream. This allows you to view multiple packets together, that are part of a TCP exchange, in the same connection.

Also, try logging into www.gmail.com or any other popular website and analyze the data traffic generated.

We will now see a demonstration of how to inject packets into a wireless network.

Time for action – packet injection

We will be using the aireplay-ng tool, which is available in Kali, for this exercise.

Follow these instructions carefully:

1. In order to do an injection test, first start Wireshark and the filter expression (wlan.bssid == <mac>) && !(wlan.fc.type_subtype == 0x08). This will ensure that we only see non-beacon packets for our lab network.

2. Now run the aireplay-ng -9 -e Wireless Lab -a <mac> wlan0mon command in a terminal.

3. Go back to Wireshark and you should see a lot of packets on the screen now. Some of these packets have been sent by aireplay-ng, which we launched, and others are from the access point Wireless Lab in response to the injected packets.

What just happened?

We just successfully injected packets into our test lab network using aireplay-ng. It is important to note that our card injected these arbitrary packets into the network without being actually connected to the access point Wireless Lab.

Have a go hero – installing Kali on VirtualBox

We will look at packet injection in greater detail in later chapters; however, feel free to explore other options of the `aireplay-ng` tool to inject packets. You can verify whether injection succeeded by using Wireshark to monitor the air.

Important note on WLAN sniffing and injection

WLANs typically operate within three different frequency ranges—2.4 GHz, 3.6 GHz, and 4.9/5.0 GHz. Not all Wi-Fi cards support all these ranges and associated bands. For instance, older Alfa cards only support IEEE 802.11b/g. This would mean that these cards cannot operate in 802.11a/n. The key here is to sniff or inject packets in a particular band; your Wi-Fi card will need to support it.

Another interesting aspect of Wi-Fi is that, in each of these bands, there are multiple channels. It is important to note that your Wi-Fi card can only be on one channel at any given moment. It is not possible to tune into multiple channels at the same time. The best analogy I can give you is your car radio. You can tune it to only one of the available channels at any given time. If you want to hear something else, you will have to change the channel. The same principle applies to WLAN sniffing. This brings us to an important conclusion— we cannot sniff all channels at the same time; we will need to select the channel that is of interest to us. What this means is that, if our access point of interest is on channel 1, we will need to set our card on channel 1.

Though we have addressed WLAN sniffing in the preceding paragraphs, the same applies to injection as well. To inject packets on a specific channel, we will need to put the card radio on that channel.

Let's now do some exercises on setting our card to specific channels, channel hopping, setting regulatory domains, power levels, and many more.

Time for action – experimenting with your adapter

Follow these instructions carefully:

1. To set the card on a particular channel, we use the `iwconfig wlan0mon channel X` commands:

```
                                    root@kali: ~
 File  Edit  View  Search  Terminal  Help
root@kali:~# iwconfig wlan0mon channel 11
root@kali:~#
root@kali:~# iwconfig wlan0mon
wlan0mon  IEEE 802.11  Mode:Monitor  Frequency:2.462 GHz  Tx-Power=20 dBm
          Retry short  long limit:2   RTS thr:off   Fragment thr:off
          Power Management:off

root@kali:~#
```

2. The `iwconfig` series of commands does not have a channel hopping mode. One could write a simple script over it to make it do so. An easier way is to use `airodump-ng` with options to either hop channels arbitrarily, use only a subset, or use only selected bands. All these options are illustrated in the following screenshot when we run `airodump-ng --help`:

```
                                    root@kali: ~
 File  Edit  View  Search  Terminal  Help
    Filter options:
        --encrypt    <suite>    : Filter APs by cipher suite
        --netmask  <netmask>    : Filter APs by mask
        --bssid      <bssid>    : Filter APs by BSSID
        --essid      <essid>    : Filter APs by ESSID
        --essid-regex <regex> : Filter APs by ESSID using a regular
                                  expression
        -a                      : Filter unassociated clients

    By default, airodump-ng hop on 2.4GHz channels.
    You can make it capture on other/specific channel(s) by using:
        --channel <channels>  : Capture on specific channels
        --band <abg>          : Band on which airodump-ng should hop
        -C     <frequencies>  : Uses these frequencies in MHz to hop
        --cswitch  <method>   : Set channel switching method
                   0          : FIFO (default)
                   1          : Round Robin
                   2          : Hop on last
        -s                    : same as --cswitch

        --help                : Displays this usage screen
root@kali:~#
```

What just happened?

We understood that both wireless sniffing and packet injection depend on the hardware support available. This means that we can only operate on bands and channels allowed by our card. Also, the wireless card radio can only be on one channel at a time. Furthermore, this means that we can only sniff or inject in one channel at a time.

Have a go hero – sniffing multiple channels

If you need to simultaneously sniff on multiple channels, you will require multiple physical Wi-Fi cards. If you can procure additional cards, then try to sniff on multiple channels simultaneously.

Pop quiz – WLAN packet sniffing and injection

Q1. Which frame types are responsible for authentication in WLANs?

1. Control
2. Management
3. Data
4. QoS

Q2. What is the name of the second monitor mode interface that can be created on `wlan0` using `airmon-ng`?

1. `wlan0mon`
2. `wlan0mon1`
3. `1mon`
4. `monb`

Q3. What is the filter expression to view all non-beacon frames in Wireshark?

1. `!(wlan.fc.type_subtype == 0x08)`
2. `wlan.fc.type_subtype == 0x08`
3. `(no beacon)`
4. `wlan.fc.type == 0x08`

Summary

In this chapter, we have made some key observations about WLAN protocols.

Management, control, and data frames are unencrypted and thus can be easily read by someone who is monitoring the airspace. It is important to note here that the data packet payload can be protected using encryption to keep it confidential. We will talk about this in the next chapter.

We can sniff the entire airspace in our vicinity by putting our card into monitor mode.

As there is no integrity protection in management and control frames, it is very easy to inject these packets by modifying them or replaying them as-is using tools such as `aireplay-ng`.

Unencrypted data packets can also be modified and replayed back to the network. If the packet is encrypted, we can still replay the packet as-is, as WLAN by design does not have packet replay protection.

In the next chapter, we will look at different authentication mechanisms that are used in WLANs such as MAC filtering and shared authentication, and understand the various security flaws in them through live demonstrations.

3
Bypassing WLAN Authentication

"A false sense of security is worse than being unsure."

– Anonymous

A false sense of security is worse than being insecure, as you may not be
prepared to face the eventuality of being hacked.

WLANs can have weak authentication schemas that can be easily broken and
bypassed. In this chapter, we will take a look at the various basic authentication
schemas used in WLANs and learn how to beat them.

In this chapter, we will take a look at the following topics:

◆ Uncovering hidden SSIDs

◆ Beating MAC filters

◆ Bypassing Open Authentication

◆ Bypassing **Shared Key Authentication (SKA)**

Hidden SSIDs

In the default configuration mode, all access points send out their SSIDs in beacon frames.
This allows clients in the vicinity to discover them easily. Hidden SSIDs is a configuration
where the access point does not broadcast its SSID in beacon frames. Thus, only clients that
know the SSID of the access point can connect to it.

Unfortunately, this measure does not provide robust security, but most network administrators think it does. Hidden SSIDs should not be considered a security measure by any stretch of the imagination. We will now take a look at how to uncover hidden SSIDs.

Time for action – uncovering hidden SSIDs

Perform the following instructions to get started:

1. Using Wireshark, if we monitor beacon frames in the Wireless Lab network, we are able to see the SSID in plain text. You should see beacon frames, as shown in the following screenshot:

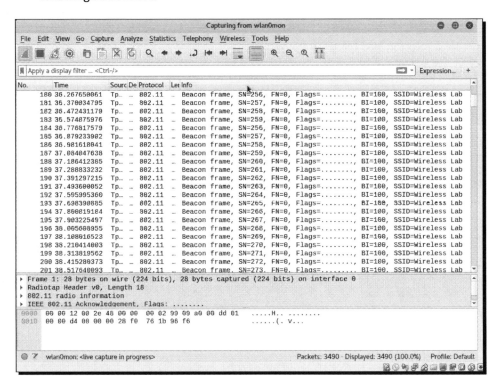

2. Configure your access point to set the `Wireless Lab` network as a hidden SSID. The configuration option to do this may differ across access points. In my case, I need to check the `Invisible` option in the **Visibility Status** option, as shown in the following screenshot:

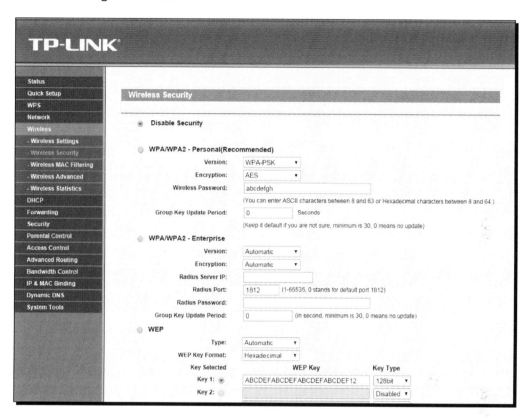

3. Now if you take a look at the Wireshark trace, you will find that the SSID `Wireless Lab` has disappeared from the beacon frames. This is what hidden SSIDs are all about:

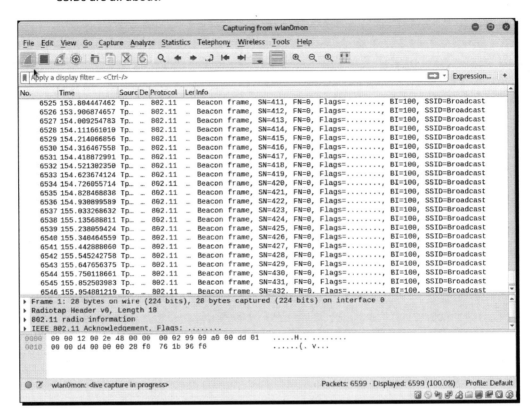

4. In order to bypass beacon frames, we will first use the passive technique of waiting for a legitimate client to connect to the access point. This will generate probe request and probe response packets that will contain the SSID of the network, thus revealing its presence:

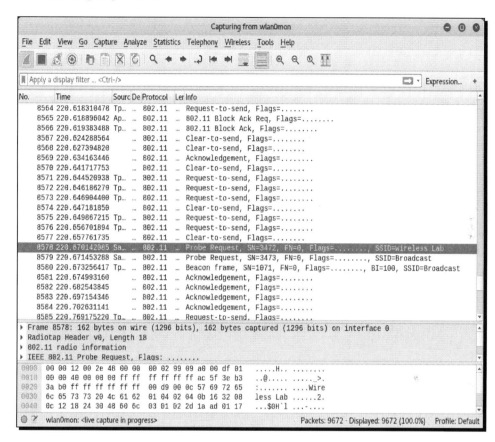

5. Alternatively, you can use the `aireplay-ng` utility to send deauthentication packets to all stations on behalf of the `Wireless Lab` access point by typing `aireplay-ng -0 5 -a <mac>  --ignore-negative wlan0mon`, where `<mac>` is the MAC address of the router. The `-0` option is used to choose a deauthentication attack, and `5` is the number of deauthentication packets to send. Finally, `-a` specifies the MAC address of the access point you are targeting:

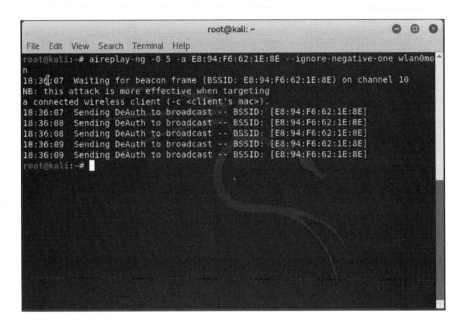

6. The preceding deauthentication packets will force all legitimate clients to disconnect and reconnect. It would be a good idea to add a filter for deauthentication packets to view them in an isolated way, which we can do with `wlan.fc.type_subtype == 0x0c`:

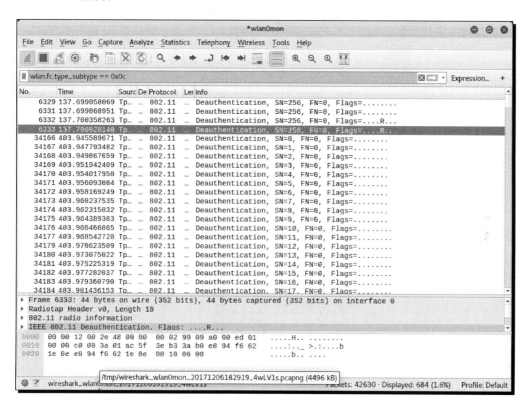

7. The probe responses from the access point will end up revealing its hidden SSID. These packets will show up on Wireshark as shown in the following screenshot. Once the legitimate clients connect back, we can see the hidden SSID using the probe request and probe response frames. You can use the filter `(wlan.bssid == <the AP MAC>) && !(wlan.fc.type_subtype == 0x08)` to monitor all non-beacon packets to and fro from the access point. The `&&` sign stands for the logical AND operator and the `!` sign stands for the logical NOT operator:

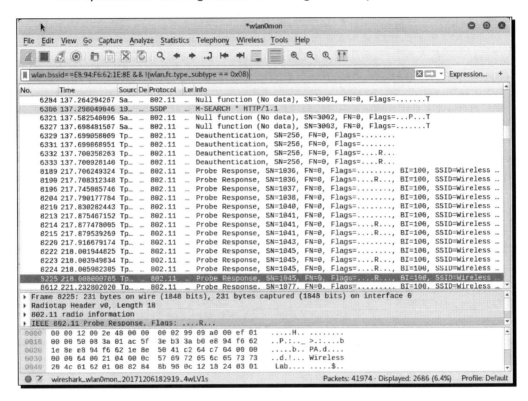

What just happened?

Even though the SSID is hidden and not broadcasted, whenever a legitimate client tries to connect to the access point, they exchange probe request and probe response packets. These packets contain the SSID of the access point. As these packets are not encrypted, they can be very easily sniffed from the air and the SSID can be found.

We will cover using probe requests for other purposes such as tracking in a later chapter.

In many cases, all clients may be already connected to the access point and there may be no probe request/response packets available in the Wireshark trace. Here, we can forcibly disconnect the clients from the access point by sending forged deauthentication packets on the air. These packets will force the clients to reconnect back to the access point, thus revealing the SSID.

Have a go hero – selecting deauthentication

In the previous exercise, we sent broadcast deauthentication packets to force reconnection of all wireless clients. Try to verify how you can selectively target individual clients using the `aireplay-ng` utility.

It is important to note that, even though we are illustrating many of these concepts using Wireshark, it is possible to orchestrate these attacks with other tools, such as the `aircrack-ng` suite as well. We encourage you to explore the entire `aircrack-ng` suite of tools and other documentation located on their website at `http://www.aircrack-ng.org`.

MAC filters

MAC filters are an age-old technique used for authentication and authorization and have their roots in the wired world. Unfortunately, they fail miserably in the wireless world.

The basic idea is to authenticate based on the MAC address of the client. The MAC filter is an identification code assigned to a network interface; a router will be able to check this code and compare it to a list of approved MACs. This list of allowed MAC addresses will be maintained by the network administrator and will be fed into the access point. We will now take a look at how easy it is to bypass MAC filters.

Time for action – beating MAC filters

Let's follow the instructions to get started:

1. Let's first configure our access point to use MAC filtering and then add the client MAC address of the victim laptop. The settings pages on my router looks as follows:

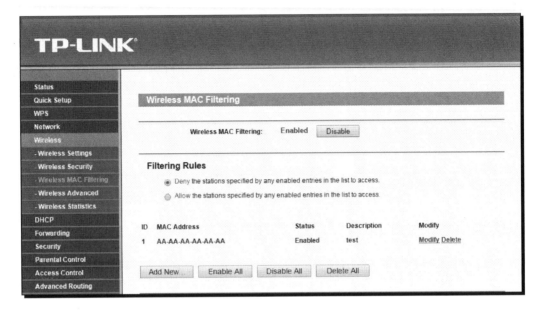

2. Once MAC filtering is enabled, only the allowed MAC address will be able to successfully authenticate with the access point. If we try to connect to the access point from a machine with a non-whitelisted MAC address, the connection will fail.

3. Behind the scenes, the access point is sending authentication failure messages to the client. The packet trace resembles the following:

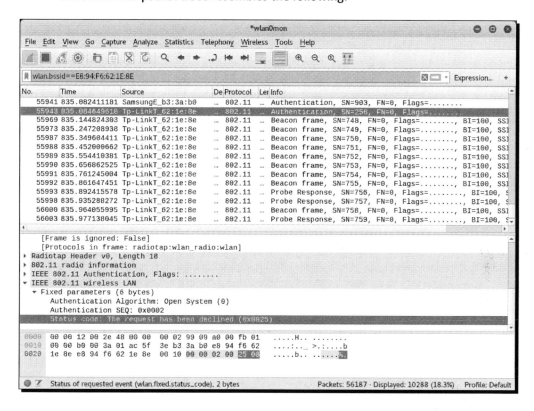

4. In order to beat MAC filters, we can use `airodump-ng` to find the MAC addresses of clients connected to the access point. We can do this by issuing the `airodump-ng -c 10 -a --bssid <mac> wlan0mon` command. By specifying the `bssid` command, we will only monitor the access point, which is of interest to us. The `-c 10` command sets the channel to `10`, where the access point is. The `-a` command ensures that, in the client section of the `airodump-ng` output, only clients associated and connected to an access point are shown. This will show us all the client MAC addresses associated with the access point:

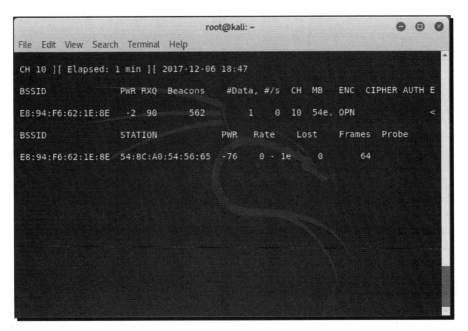

5. Once we find a whitelisted client's MAC address, we can spoof the MAC address of the client using the `macchanger` utility, which ships with Kali. You can use the `macchanger -m <mac> wlan0mon` command to get this done. The MAC address you specify with the `-m` command option is the new spoofed MAC address for the `wlan0mon` interface:

```
                              root@kali: ~                    ●  ●  ✖
File  Edit  View  Search  Terminal  Help
root@kali:~# ifconfig wlan0mon down
root@kali:~# macchanger -m 54:8C:A0:54:56:65 wlan0mon
Current MAC:    ac:5f:3e:b3:3a:b0 (unknown)
Permanent MAC: 00:c0:ca:95:4c:8c (ALFA, INC.)
New MAC:        54:8c:a0:54:56:65 (unknown)
root@kali:~# ifconfig wlan0mon up
root@kali:~#
```

6. As you can clearly see, we are now able to connect to the access point after spoofing the MAC address of a whitelisted client.

What just happened?

We monitored the air using `airodump-ng` and found the MAC address of legitimate clients connected to the wireless network. We then used the `macchanger` utility to change our wireless card's MAC address to match the client's. This fooled the access point into believing that we were the legitimate client, and it allowed us access to its wireless network.

You are encouraged to explore the different options of the `airodump-ng` utility by going through the documentation on their website at `http://www.aircrack-ng.org/doku.php?id=airodump-ng`.

Open Authentication

The term Open Authentication is almost a misnomer, as it actually provides no authentication at all. When an access point is configured to use Open Authentication, it will successfully authenticate all clients that connect to it.

We will now do an exercise to authenticate and connect to an access point using Open Authentication.

Time for action – bypassing Open Authentication

Let's now take a look at how to bypass Open Authentication:

1. We will first set our lab access point Wireless Lab to use Open Authentication. On my access point, this is simply done by setting **Security Mode** to **Disable Security**:

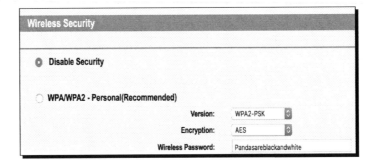

2. We then connect to this access point using the `iwconfig wlan0 essid Wireless Lab` command and verify that the connection has succeeded and that we are connected to the access point.

3. Note that we did not have to supply any username/password/passphrase to get through Open Authentication.

What just happened?

This is probably the simplest exercise so far. As you saw, there is no barrier to connecting to an Open Authentication network and connecting to the access point.

Shared Key Authentication

SKA uses a shared secret such as the WEP key to authenticate the client. The exact exchange of information is illustrated in the following screenshot (taken from www.netgear.com):

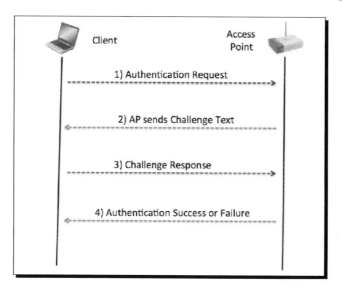

The wireless client sends an authentication request to the access point, which responds back with a challenge. The client now needs to encrypt this challenge with the shared key and send it back to the access point, which decrypts this to check whether it can recover the original challenge text. If it succeeds, the client successfully authenticates; if not, it sends an authentication failed message.

The security problem here is that an attacker passively listening to this entire communication by sniffing the air has access to both the plain text challenge and the encrypted challenge. He can apply the XOR operation to retrieve the keystream. This keystream can be used to encrypt any future challenge sent by the access point without needing to know the actual key.

The most common form of shared authentication is known as **Wired Equivalent Privacy (WEP)**. It is easy to break, and numerous tools have been created over time to facilitate the cracking of WEP networks.

In this exercise, we will learn how to sniff the air to retrieve the challenge and the encrypted challenge, retrieve the keystream, and use it to authenticate to the access point without needing the shared key.

Time for action – bypassing shared authentication

Bypassing shared authentication is a bit more challenging than the previous exercises, so follow the steps carefully:

1. Let's first set up shared authentication for our Wireless Lab network. I have done this on my access point by setting the security mode as **WEP** and **Authentication** as **Shared Key**:

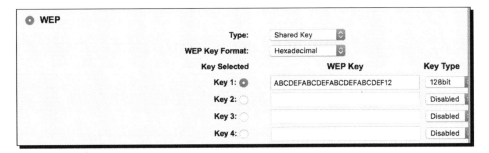

2. Let's now connect a legitimate client to this network using the shared key we have set in step 1.

3. In order to bypass SKA, we will first start sniffing packets between the access point and its clients. However, we would also like to log the entire shared authentication exchange. To do this, we use the `airodump-ng` utility using the `airodump-ng wlan0mon -c 11 --bssid <mac> -w keystream` command. The `-w` option, which is new here, requests `airodump-ng` to store the packets in a file whose name is prefixed with the word `keystream`. Incidentally, it might be a good idea to store different sessions of packet captures in different files. This allows you to analyze them long after the trace has been collected:

4. We can either wait for a legitimate client to connect to the access point or force a reconnect using the deauthentication technique used previously. Once a client connects and the SKA succeeds, `airodump-ng` will capture this exchange automatically by sniffing the air. An indication that the capture has succeeded is when the AUTH column reads WEP.

5. The captured keystream is stored in a file prefixed with the word `keystream` in the current directory. In my case, the name of the file is `keystream-01-00-21-91-D2-8E-25.xor`.

6. If this doesn't work, you can use `aireplay-ng -4 -h <Connected Device MAC> -a <AP BSSID> wlan0mon` to generate an `.xor` file. This requires a connected device to be on the target WEP protected network and will generate packets spoofing their MAC address to identify the XOR stream and key.

7. In order to fake a SKA, we will use the `aireplay-ng` tool. We run the `aireplay-ng -1 0 -e "Wireless Lab" -y keystream-01-00-21-91-D2-8E-25.xor -a <mac> -h AA:AA:AA:AA:AA:AA wlan0mon` command. This `aireplay-ng` command uses the keystream we just retrieved and tries to authenticate with the access point with the SSID, `Wireless Lab` and the MAC address, `00:21:91:D2:8E:25`, and uses an arbitrary client MAC address, `AA:AA:AA:AA:AA:AA`.

8. Fire up Wireshark and sniff all packets of interest by applying a `wlan.addr ==`
   `AA:AA:AA:AA:AA:AA` filter. We can verify this using Wireshark. You should see a
   trace on the Wireshark screen, as shown in the following screenshot:

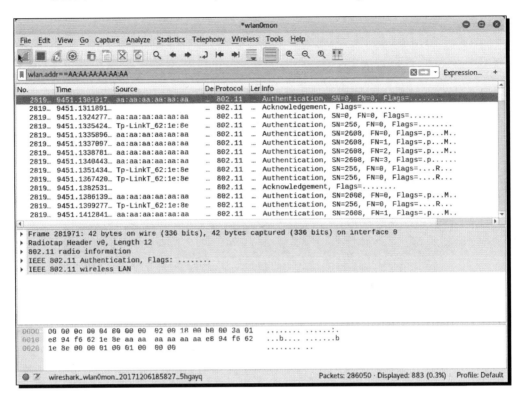

9. The first packet is the authentication request sent by the `aireplay-ng` tool to the access point:

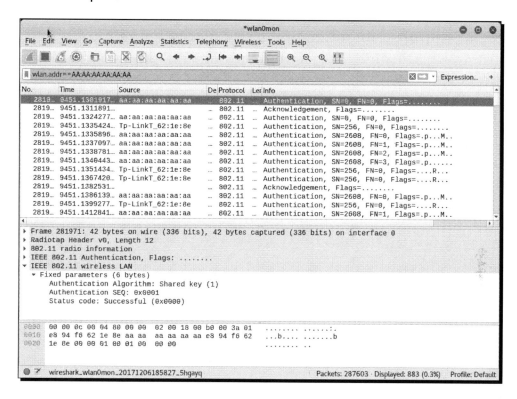

10. The second packet consists of the access point sending the client challenge text, as shown in the following screenshot:

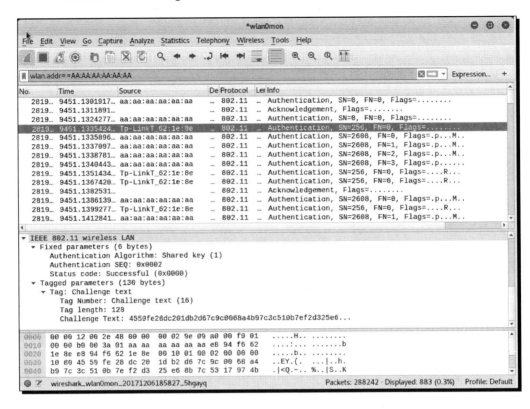

11. In the third packet, the tool sends the encrypted challenge to the access point:

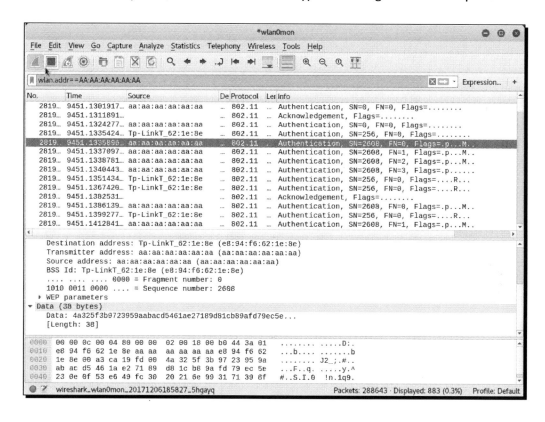

12. As the `aireplay-ng` tool used the derived keystream for encryption, the authentication succeeds and the access point sends a success message in the fourth packet:

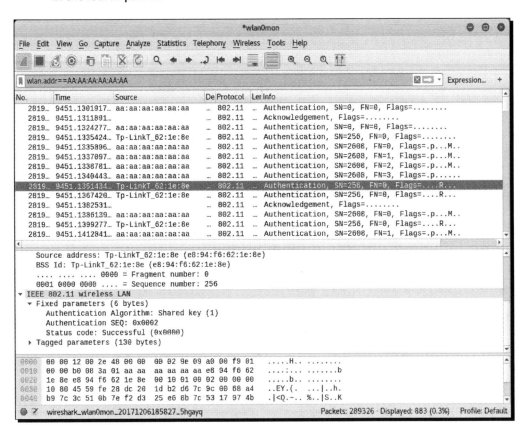

13. After the authentication succeeds, the tool fakes an association with the access point, which succeeds as well. If you check the wireless logs in your access point's administrative interface, you should now see a wireless client with the MAC address, AA:AA:AA:AA:AA:AA connected:

What just happened?

We were successful in deriving the keystream from a shared authentication exchange, and we used it to fake an authentication to the access point.

Have a go hero – filling up the access point's tables

Access points have a maximum client count after which they start refusing connections. By writing a simple wrapper over `aireplay-ng`, it is possible to automate and send hundreds of connection requests from random MAC addresses to the access point. This will end up filling the internal tables and once the maximum client count is reached, the access point will stop accepting new connections. This is typically what is called a **Denial of Service (DoS)** attack and can force the router to reboot or make it dysfunctional. This can lead to all the wireless clients being disconnected and being unable to use the authorized network.

Check whether you can verify this in your lab!

Pop quiz – WLAN authentication

Q1. How can you force a wireless client to reconnect to the access point?

1. By sending a deauthentication packet
2. By rebooting the client
3. By rebooting the access point
4. All of the above

Q2. What does Open Authentication do?

1. It provides decent security
2. It provides no security
3. It requires the use of encryption
4. None of the above

Q3. How does breaking SKA work?

1. By deriving the keystream from the packets
2. By deriving the encryption key
3. By sending deauthentication packets to the access point
4. By rebooting the access point

Summary

In this chapter, we learnt about WLAN authentication. Hidden SSIDs are a security-through-obscurity feature and are relatively simple to beat. MAC address filters do not provide any security, as MAC addresses can be sniffed from the air from the wireless packets. This is possible because the MAC addresses are unencrypted in the packet. Open Authentication provides no real authentication at all. SKA is a bit tricky to beat but, with the help of the right tools, we can derive the store and the keystream, using which it is possible to answer all future challenges sent by the access point. The result is that we can authenticate without needing to know the actual key.

In the next chapter, we will take a look at different WLAN encryption mechanisms—WEP, WPA, and WPA2—and look at the insecurities that plague them.

4
WLAN Encryption Flaws

"640K is more memory than anyone will ever need."

– Bill Gates, Founder, Microsoft

Even with the best of intentions, the future is always unpredictable. The WLAN committee designed WEP and then WPA to be foolproof encryption mechanisms but, over time, both these mechanisms had flaws that have been widely publicized and exploited in the real world.

WLAN encryption mechanisms have had a long history of being vulnerable to cryptographic attacks. It started with WEP in early 2000, which eventually was completely broken. In recent times, WPA has been proven to contain multiple flaws that have been addressed and readdressed. Even though there is no public attack available currently to break WPA in all general conditions, there are attacks that are feasible under special circumstances.

In this chapter, we will take a look at the following topics:

- ◆ Different encryption schemas in WLANs
- ◆ Cracking WEP encryption
- ◆ Cracking WPA encryption

WLAN encryption

WLANs transmit data over the air and thus there is an inherent need to protect data confidentiality. This is best done using encryption. The WLAN committee (IEEE 802.11) formulated the following protocols for data encryption:

- ◆ **Wired Equivalent Privacy (WEP)**
- ◆ **Wi-Fi Protected Access (WPA)**
- ◆ **Wi-Fi Protected Access v2 (WPA2)**

In this chapter, we will take a look at each of these encryption protocols and demonstrate various attacks against them.

WEP encryption

The WEP protocol was known to be flawed as early as 2000 but, surprisingly, it is still present in a lot of organizations and access points still ship with WEP enabled capabilities.

There are many cryptographic weaknesses in WEP and they were discovered by Walker, Arbaugh, Fluhrer, Martin, Shamir, KoreK, and many others. Evaluation of WEP from a cryptographic standpoint is not required for a basic understanding of how to break it. In this section, we will take a look at how to break WEP encryption using readily available tools on Kali Linux. This includes the entire `aircrack-ng` suite of tools: `airmon-ng`, `aireplay-ng`, `airodump-ng`, `aircrack-ng`, and others.

The fundamental weakness in WEP is its use of RC4 and a short IV value that is recycled every 224 frames. While this may appear to be a large number, there is a 50 percent chance of four IV reuses every 5,000 packets. To use this to our advantage, we generate a large amount of traffic so that we can increase the likelihood of IVs that have been reused and thus compare two cipher texts encrypted with the same IV and key.

Let's now first set up WEP in our test lab and see how we can break it.

Time for action – cracking WEP

Follow the given instructions to get started:

1. Let's first connect to our access point Wireless Lab and go to the settings area that deals with wireless encryption mechanisms.

2. On my access point, this can be done by setting the **Security Mode** to **WEP**. We will also need to set the WEP key length. As shown in the following screenshot, I have set WEP to use **128bit** keys. I have set the default key to WEP **Key 1** and the value in hex to `abcdefabcdefabcdefabcdef12` as the 128-bit WEP key. You can set this to whatever you choose:

3. Once the settings are applied, the access point should now be offering WEP as the encryption mechanism of choice. Let's now set up the attacker machine.

4. Let's bring up `wlan0` by issuing the following command:

```
ifconfig wlan0 up
```

5. Then, we will run the following command:

```
airmon-ng start wlan0
```

6. This is done to create `wlan0mon`, a monitor mode interface, as shown in the following screenshot. Verify that the `wlan0mon` interface has been created using the `ifconfig` command:

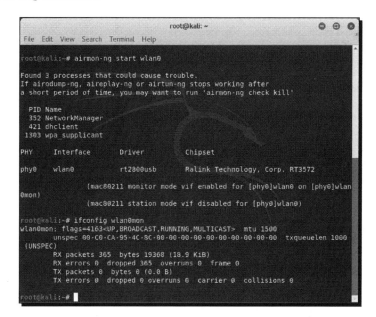

7. Let's run `airodump-ng` to locate our lab access point using the following command:

    ```
    airodump-ng wlan0mon
    ```

8. As you can see in the following screenshot, we are able to see the `Wireless Lab` access point running WEP:

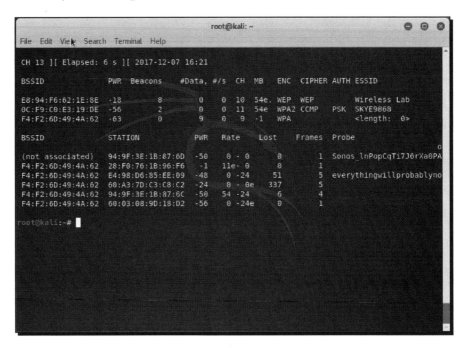

9. For this exercise, we are only interested in the `Wireless Lab` network, so we can fine-tune our command to only see packets for this network:

    ```
    airodump-ng --bssid <Your AP MAC> --channel <whatever channel it's on> --write WEPCrackingDemo wlan0mon
    ```

    An example command line is shown in the following screenshot:

10. We will request `airodump-ng` to save the packets into a `pcap` file using the `--write` flag:

11. Now, let's connect our wireless client to the access point and use the WEP key as `abcdefabcdefabcdefabcdef12`. Once the client has successfully connected, `airodump-ng` should report it on the screen:

12. If you execute `ls` in the same directory, you will be able to see files prefixed with `WEPCrackingDemo-*`, as shown in the following screenshot. These are traffic dump files created by `airodump-ng`:

13. If you notice the `airodump-ng` screen, there are very few data packets listed under #Data (only 35):

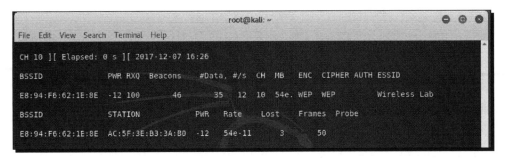

14. In WEP cracking, we need a large number of data packets, encrypted with the same key to exploit weaknesses in the protocol. So, we will have to force the network to produce more data packets. To do this, we will use the `aireplay-ng` tool.

15. We will capture ARP packets on the wireless network using `aireplay-ng` and inject them back into the network to simulate ARP responses. We will be starting `aireplay-ng` in a separate window, as shown in the next screenshot. Replaying these packets a few thousand times, we will generate a lot of data traffic on the network. Even though `aireplay-ng` does not know the WEP key, it is able to identify the ARP packets by looking at the size of the packets. ARP is a fixed header protocol; thus, the size of the ARP packets can be easily determined and can be used to identify them even within encrypted traffic. We will run `aireplay-ng` with the options that are discussed next. The `-3` option is for ARP replay, `-b` specifies the BSSID of our network, and `-h` specifies the client MAC address that we are spoofing. Don't forget to add the adapter to use. We need to do this, as replay attacks will only work for authenticated and associated client MAC addresses:

16. Very soon you should see that `aireplay-ng` was able to sniff ARP packets and started replaying them into the network. If you encounter channel-related errors as I did, append `--ignore-negative-one` to your command, as shown in the following screenshot:

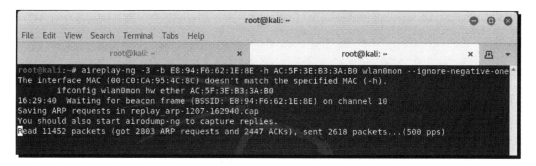

17. At this point, `airodump-ng` will also start registering a lot of data packets. All these sniffed packets are being stored in the `WEPCrackingDemo-*` files that we saw previously:

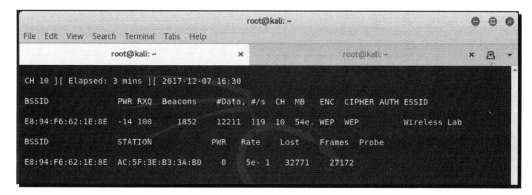

18. Now, let's start with the actual cracking part! Fire up `aircrack-ng` with the option `WEPCRackingDemo-0*.cap` in a new window. This will start the `aircrack-ng` software and it will begin working on cracking the WEP key using the data packets in the file. Note that it is a good idea to have `airodump-ng` collect the WEP packets, `aireplay-ng` do the replay attack, and `aircrack-ng` attempt to crack the WEP key based on the captured packets, all at the same time. In this experiment, all of them are open in separate windows:

19. Your screen should look like the following screenshot when Aircrack-ng is working on the packets to crack the WEP key:

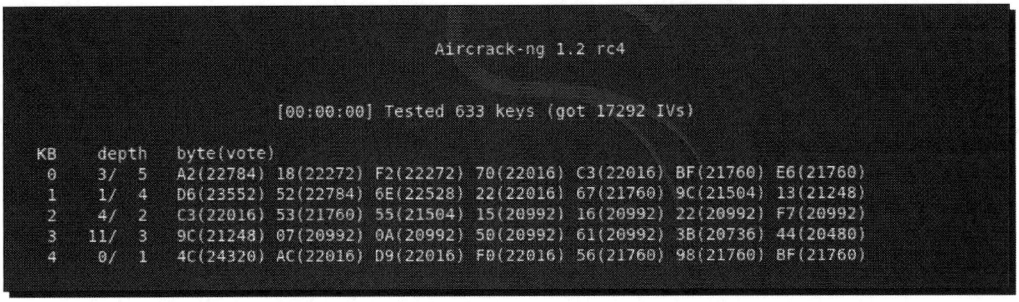

```
                            Aircrack-ng 1.2 rc4


                    [00:00:00] Tested 633 keys (got 17292 IVs)

 KB    depth   byte(vote)
  0    3/  5   A2(22784) 18(22272) F2(22272) 70(22016) C3(22016) BF(21760) E6(21760)
  1    1/  4   D6(23552) 52(22784) 6E(22528) 22(22016) 67(21760) 9C(21504) 13(21248)
  2    4/  2   C3(22016) 53(21760) 55(21504) 15(20992) 16(20992) 22(20992) F7(20992)
  3   11/  3   9C(21248) 07(20992) 0A(20992) 50(20992) 61(20992) 3B(20736) 44(20480)
  4    0/  1   4C(24320) AC(22016) D9(22016) F0(22016) 56(21760) 98(21760) BF(21760)
```

20. The number of data packets required to crack the key is nondeterministic, but generally in the order of a hundred thousand or more. On a fast network (or using `aireplay-ng`), this should take 5-10 minutes at most. You may need to restart this process several times.

21. Once enough data packets have been captured and processed, `aircrack-ng` should be able to break the key. Once it does, it proudly displays it in the terminal and exits, as shown in the following screenshot:

```
Starting PTW attack with 100449 ivs.



                            Aircrack-ng 1.2 rc4


                    [00:00:00] Tested 691 keys (got 98734 IVs)

 KB    depth   byte(vote)
  0    7/  8   C7(108288) C3(107776) BF(107520) E6(107520) 78(107264) 41(107008) AC(107008)
  1    6/  1   BD(108800) 22(108288) 6F(108288) 6E(108032) 31(107776) 27(107264) 77(107008)
  2   15/  2   5C(106496) 34(105728) 7E(105728) E1(105728) 5B(105472) 8E(105472) 89(105216)
  3    0/  4   12(133120) EC(110336) 17(109824) 99(109824) 13(109568) 18(109312) 04(109056)
  4    0/  2   DF(136192) F0(113408) 4F(112128) D7(111104) BF(109312) B5(109056) 0B(108544)

        KEY FOUND! [ AB:CD:EF:AB:CD:EF:AB:CD:EF:AB:CD:EF:12 ]
        Decrypted correctly: 100%


root@kali:~#
```

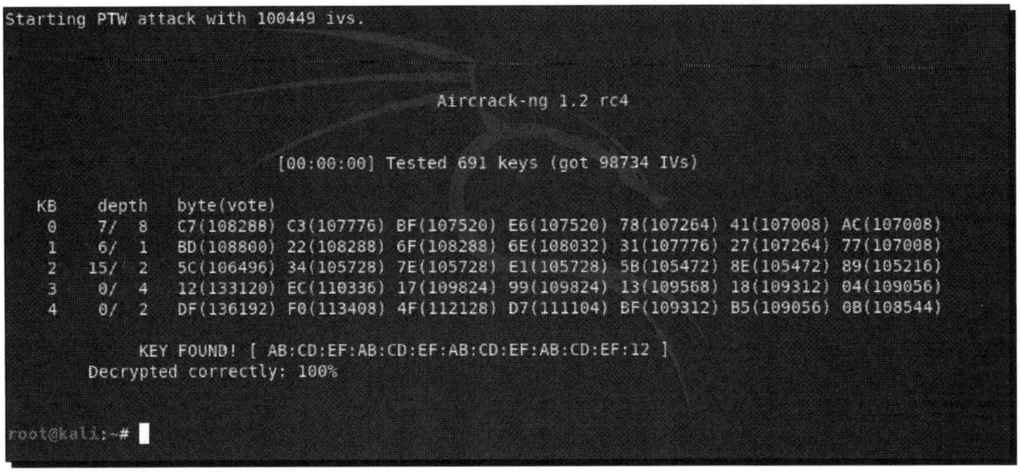

22. It is important to note that WEP is totally flawed and any WEP key (no matter how complex) will be cracked by `aircrack-ng`. The only requirement is that a large enough number of data packets, encrypted with this key, are made available to `aircrack-ng`.

What just happened?

We set up WEP in our lab and successfully cracked the WEP key. In order to do this, we first waited for a legitimate client of the network to connect to the access point. After this, we used the `aireplay-ng` tool to replay ARP packets into the network. This caused the network to send ARP replay packets, thus greatly increasing the number of data packets sent over the air. We then used the `aircrack-ng` tool to crack the WEP key by analyzing cryptographic weaknesses in these data packets.

Note that we can also fake an authentication to the access point using the **Shared Key Authentication (SKA)** bypass technique we learned in the last chapter. This can come in handy if the legitimate client leaves the network. This will ensure that we can spoof an authentication and association and continue to send our replayed packets into the network.

Have a go hero – fake authentication with WEP cracking

In the previous exercise, if the legitimate client had suddenly logged off the network, we would not have been able to replay the packets as the access point will refuse to accept packets from unassociated clients.

Your challenge will be to fake an authentication and association using the SKA bypass we learnt in the last chapter, while WEP cracking is going on. Log off the legitimate client from the network and verify that you are still able to inject packets into the network and whether the access point accepts and responds to them.

WPA/WPA2

WPA (or WPA v1 as it is referred to sometimes) primarily uses the **Temporal Key Integrity Protocol (TKIP)** encryption algorithm. TKIP was aimed at improving WEP, without requiring completely new hardware to run it. WPA2 in contrast mandatorily uses the AES-CCMP algorithm for encryption, which is much more powerful and robust than TKIP.

Both WPA and WPA2 allow either EAP-based authentication, using RADIUS servers (Enterprise) or a **Pre-Shared Key (PSK)** (personal)-based authentication schema.

WPA/WPA2 PSK is vulnerable to a dictionary attack. The inputs required for this attack are the four-way WPA handshake between client and access point, and a wordlist that contains common passphrases. Then, using tools such as `aircrack-ng`, we can try to crack the WPA/WPA2 PSK passphrase.

An illustration of the four-way handshake is shown in the following screenshot:

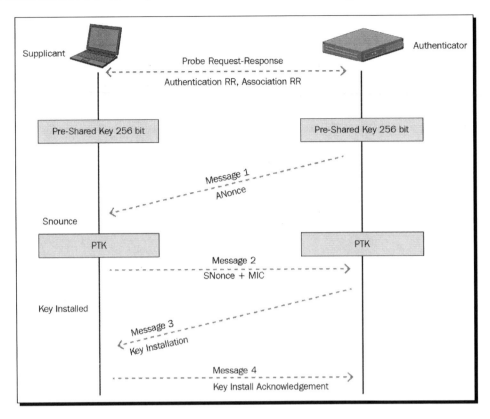

The way WPA/WPA2 PSK works is that it derives the per-session key, called the **Pairwise Transient Key (PTK)**, using the PSK and five other parameters—SSID of network, **Authenticator Nonce (ANonce)**, **Supplicant Nonce (SNonce)**, Authenticator MAC address (access point MAC), and Suppliant MAC address (Wi-Fi client MAC). This key is then used to encrypt all data between the access point and client.

An attacker who is eavesdropping on this entire conversation by sniffing the air can get all five parameters mentioned in the previous paragraph. The only thing he does not have is the PSK. So, how is the PSK created? It is derived by using the WPA-PSK passphrase supplied by the user, along with the SSID. The combination of both of these is sent through the **Password-Based Key Derivation Function (PBKDF2)**, which outputs the 256-bit shared key.

In a typical WPA/WPA2 PSK dictionary attack, the attacker would use a large dictionary of possible passphrases with the attack tool. The tool would derive the 256-bit PSK from each of the passphrases and use it with the other parameters, described earlier, to create the PTK. The PTK will be used to verify the **Message Integrity Check (MIC)** in one of the handshake packets. If it matches, then the guessed passphrase from the dictionary was correct; if not, it was incorrect.

Eventually, if the authorized network passphrase exists in the dictionary, it will be identified. This is exactly how WPA/WPA2 PSK cracking works! The following diagram illustrates the steps involved:

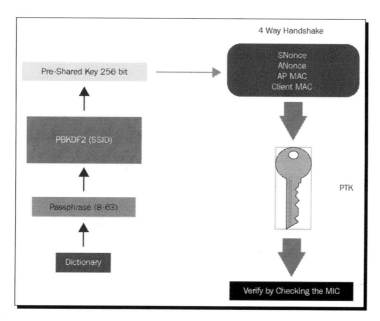

In the next exercise, we will take a look at how to crack a WPA PSK wireless network. The exact same steps will be involved in cracking a WPA2-PSK network using CCMP (AES) as well.

Time for action – cracking WPA-PSK weak passphrase

Follow the given instructions to get started:

1. Let's first connect to our access point `Wireless Lab` and set the access point to use WPA-PSK. We will set the WPA-PSK passphrase to `abcdefgh` so that it is vulnerable to a dictionary attack:

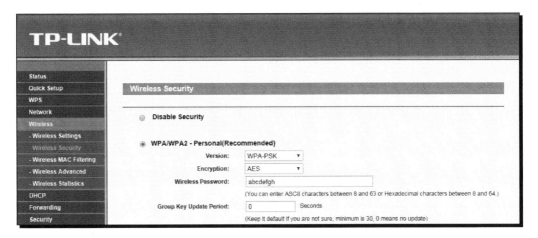

2. We start `airodump-ng` with the following command so that it starts capturing and storing all packets for our network:

    ```
    airodump-ng --bssid 00:21:91:D2:8E:25 --channel 11 --write
    WPACrackingDemo wlan0mon
    ```

    The following screenshot shows the output:

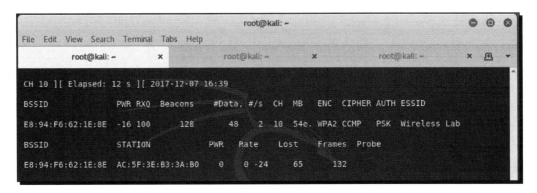

3. Now, we can wait for a new client to connect to the access point so that we can capture the four-way WPA handshake, or we can send a broadcast deauthentication packet to force clients to reconnect. We do the latter to speed things up. The same thing can happen again with the unknown channel error. Again, use `--ignore-negative-one`. This can also require more than one attempt:

4. As soon as we capture a WPA handshake, the `airodump-ng` tool will indicate it in the top-right corner of the screen with a WPA handshake followed by the access point's BSSID:

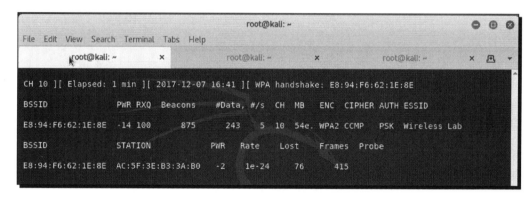

5. If you are using `--ignore-negative-one`, the tool may replace the WPA handshake with a fixed channel message. Just keep an eye out for a quick flash of a WPA handshake. If we check our working directory, we should see that a `.cap` file has been generated:

6. We can stop the `airodump-ng` utility now. Let's open up the capture file in Wireshark and view the four-way handshake. Your Wireshark terminal should look like the following screenshot. I have selected the first packet of the four-way handshake in the trace file in the screenshot. The handshake packets are the one whose protocol is `EAPOL`. You can filter this by typing `eapol` into the filter bar:

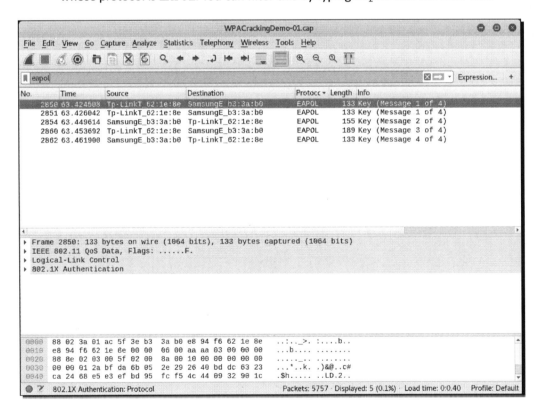

7. Now, we will start the actual key cracking exercise! For this, we need a dictionary of common words. Kali ships with many dictionary files in the `metasploit` folder located as shown in the following screenshot. It is important to note that, in WPA cracking, you are just as good as your dictionary. Kali ships with some dictionaries, but these may be insufficient. Passwords that people choose depend on a lot of things. This includes things such as which country users live in, common names and phrases in that region, the security awareness of the users, and a host of other things. It may be a good idea to aggregate country- and region-specific wordlists, when undertaking a penetration test:

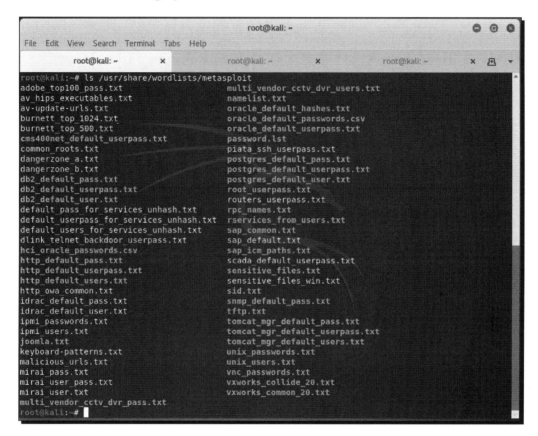

8. We will now invoke the `aircrack-ng` utility with the `pcap` file as the input and a link to the dictionary file, as shown in the following screenshot. I have used `nmap.lst` which can be found in `/usr/share/wordlists/`, as shown in the terminal:

9. The `aircrack-ng` utility uses the dictionary file to try various combinations of passphrases and tries to crack the key. If the passphrase is present in the dictionary file, it will eventually crack it and your screen will look similar to the one in the screenshot:

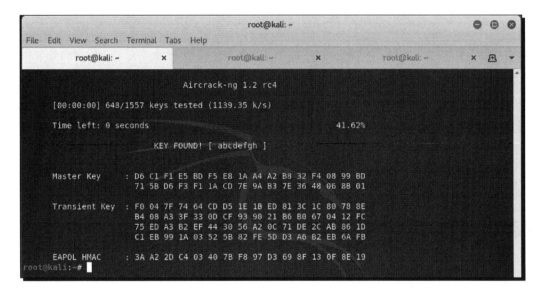

10. Please note that, as this is a dictionary attack, the prerequisite is that the passphrase must be present in the dictionary file you are supplying to `aircrack-ng`. If the passphrase is not present in the dictionary, the attack will fail!

What just happened?

We set up WPA-PSK on our access point with a common passphrase: `abcdefgh`.
We then use a deauthentication attack to have legitimate clients reconnect to the access point. When we reconnect, we capture the four-way WPA handshake between the access point and the client.

As WPA-PSK is vulnerable to a dictionary attack, we feed the capture file that contains the WPA four-way handshake and a list of common passphrases (in the form of a wordlist) to `aircrack-ng`. As the passphrase abcdefgh is present in the wordlist, `aircrack-ng` is able to crack the WPA-PSK shared passphrase. It is very important to note again that, in WPA dictionary-based cracking, you are just as good as the dictionary you have. Thus, it is important to compile a large and elaborate dictionary before you begin. Though Kali ships with its own dictionary, it may be insufficient at times and might need more words, especially taking into account the localization factor.

Have a go hero – trying WPA-PSK cracking with Cowpatty

Cowpatty is a tool that can also crack a WPA-PSK passphrase using a dictionary attack. This tool is included with Kali. I leave it as an exercise for you to use Cowpatty to crack the WPA-PSK passphrase.

Also, set an uncommon passphrase that is not present in the dictionary and try the attack again. You will now be unsuccessful in cracking the passphrase with both Aircrack-ng and Cowpatty.

It is important to note that the same attack applies even to a WPA2 PSK network. I encourage you to verify this independently.

Speeding up WPA/WPA2 PSK cracking

As we have already seen in the previous section, if we have the correct passphrase in our dictionary, cracking WPA-Personal will work every time like a charm. So, why don't we just create a large elaborate dictionary of millions of common passwords and phrases people use? This would help us a lot and most of the time, we would end up cracking the passphrase. It all sounds great but we are missing one key component here—the time taken. One of the more CPU and time-consuming calculations is that of the PSK using the PSK passphrase and the SSID through the PBKDF2. This function hashes the combination of both over 4,096 times before outputting the 256-bit PSK. The next step in cracking involves using this key along with parameters in the four-way handshake and verifying against the MIC in the handshake. This step is computationally inexpensive. Also, the parameters will vary in the handshake every time and hence, this step cannot be precomputed. Thus, to speed up the cracking process, we need to make the calculation of the PSK from the passphrase as fast as possible.

We can speed this up by precalculating the PSK, also called the **Pairwise Master Key** (PMK) in 802.11 standard parlance. It is important to note that, as the SSID is also used to calculate the PMK, with the same passphrase and with a different SSID, we will end up with a different PMK. Thus, the PMK depends on both the passphrase and the SSID.

In the next exercise, we will take a look at how to precalculate the PMK and use it for WPA/WPA2 PSK cracking.

Time for action – speeding up the cracking process

We can proceed with the following steps:

1. We can pre-calculate the PMK for a given SSID and wordlist using the `genpmk` tool with the following command:

    ```
    genpmk -f <chosen wordlist> -d PMK-Wireless-Lab -s "Wireless Lab"
    ```

    This creates the `PMK-Wireless-Lab` file containing the pregenerated PMK:

    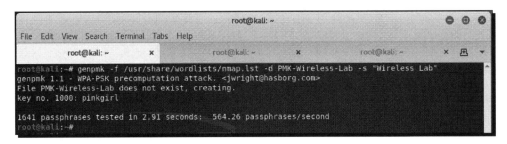

2. We now create a WPA-PSK network with the passphrase `abcdefgh` (present in the dictionary we used) and capture a WPA-handshake for that network as we did with the previous exercise; alternatively, use the files we used previously. We now use Cowpatty to crack the WPA passphrase, as shown in the following screenshot:

    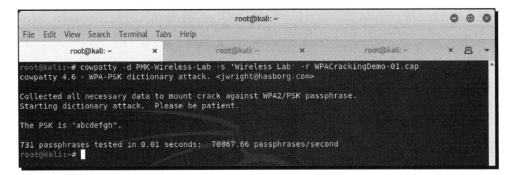

    It takes approximately 7.18 seconds for Cowpatty to crack the key, using the precalculated PMKs.

3. We now use `aircrack-ng` with the same dictionary file, and the cracking process takes over 22 minutes. This shows how much we are gaining because of the precalculation.

What just happened?

We looked at various different tools and techniques to speed up WPA/WPA2-PSK cracking. The whole idea is to precalculate the PMK for a given SSID and a list of passphrases in our dictionary.

Decrypting WEP and WPA packets

In all the exercises we have done till now, we cracked the WEP and WPA keys using various techniques. What do we do with this information? The first step is to decrypt data packets we have captured using these keys.

In the next exercise, we will decrypt the WEP and WPA packets in the same trace file that we captured over the air, using the keys we cracked.

Time for action – decrypting WEP and WPA packets

We can proceed with the following steps:

1. We will decrypt packets from the WEP capture file we created earlier: `WEPCrackingDemo-01.cap`. For this, we will use another tool in the Aircrack-ng suite called `airdecap-ng`. We will run the following command, as shown in the following screenshot, using the WEP key we cracked previously:

    airdecap-ng -w abcdefabcdefabcdefabcdef12 WEPCrackingDemo-01.cap

2. The decrypted files are stored in a file named `WEPCrackingDemo-01-dec.cap`. We use the `tshark` utility to view the first ten packets in the file. Please note that you may see something different based on what you captured:

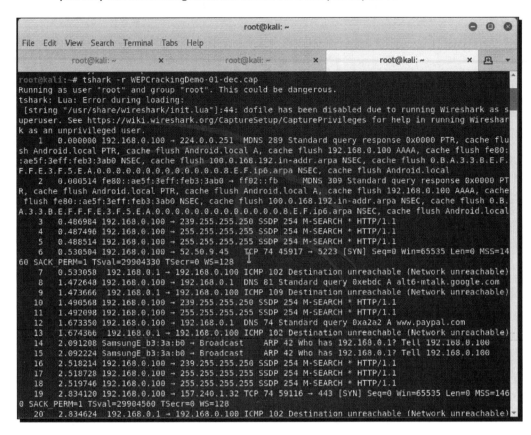

3. WPA/WPA2 PSK will work in exactly the same way as with WEP, using the `airdecap-ng` utility, as shown in the following screenshot, with the following command:

```
airdecap-ng -p abcdefgh WPACrackingDemo-01.cap -e "Wireless Lab"
```

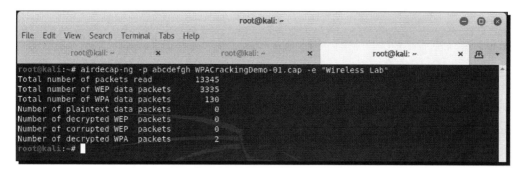

What just happened?

We just saw how we can decrypt WEP and WPA/WPA2-PSK encrypted packets using `airdecap-ng`. It is interesting to note that we can do the same using Wireshark. We would encourage you to explore how this can be done by consulting the Wireshark documentation.

Connecting to WEP and WPA networks

We can also connect to the authorized network after we have cracked the network key. This can come in handy during penetration testing. Logging onto the authorized network with the cracked key is the ultimate proof you can provide to your client that his network is insecure.

Time for action – connecting to a WEP network

We can proceed with the following steps:

1. Use the `iwconfig` utility to connect to a WEP network, once you have the key. In a past exercise, we broke the WEP key—`abcdefabcdefabcdefabcdef12`:

```
root@kali:~# iwconfig wlan0 essid "Wireless Lab" key ABCDEFABCDEFABCDEFABCDEF12
root@kali:~#
root@kali:~# iwconfig wlan0
wlan0     IEEE 802.11  ESSID:"Wireless Lab"
          Mode:Managed  Frequency:2.457 GHz  Access Point: Not-Associated
          Tx-Power=20 dBm
          Retry short  long limit:2   RTS thr:off   Fragment thr:off
          Encryption key:ABCD-EFAB-CDEF-ABCD-EFAB-CDEF-12
          Power Management:off

root@kali:~#
```

What just happened?

We saw how to connect to a WEP network.

Time for action – connecting to a WPA network

We can proceed with the following steps:

1. In the case of WPA, the matter is a bit more complicated. The `iwconfig` utility cannot be used with WPA/WPA2 Personal and Enterprise, as it does not support it. We will use a new tool called `wpa_supplicant` for this lab. To use `WPA_supplicant` for a network, we will need to create a configuration file, as shown in the following screenshot. We will name this file `wpa-supp.conf`:

2. We will then invoke the `wpa_supplicant` utility with the following command:

```
wpa_supplicant -D wext -i wlan0 -c wpa-supp.conf
```

3. This will connect the device to the WPA network we just cracked. Once the connection is successful, `wpa_supplicant` will give you the message: **Connection to XXXX completed**.

4. For both the WEP and WPA networks, once you are connected, you can use `dhclient` to grab a DHCP address from the network by typing `dhclient3 wlan0`.

What just happened?

The default Wi-Fi utility `iwconfig` cannot be used to connect to WPA/WPA2 networks. The de-facto tool for this is `wpa_supplicant`. In this lab, we saw how we can use it to connect to a WPA network.

Pop quiz – WLAN encryption flaws

Q1. What packets are used for packet replay?

1. Deauthentication packet

2. Associated packet

3. Encrypted ARP packet

4. None of the above

Q2. When can WEP be cracked?

1. Always

2. Only if a weak key/passphrase is chosen

3. Under special circumstances only

4. Only if the access point runs old software

Summary

In this chapter, we learnt about WLAN encryption. WEP is flawed and no matter what the WEP key is, with enough data packet samples: it is always possible to crack WEP. WPA/WPA2 is cryptographically un-crackable currently; however, under special circumstances, such as when a weak passphrase is chosen in WPA/WPA2-PSK, it is possible to retrieve the passphrase using dictionary attacks.

In the next chapter, we will take a look at different attacks on the WLAN infrastructure, such as rogue access points, evil twins, bit-flipping attacks, and so on.

5

Attacks on the WLAN Infrastructure

"Thus, what is of supreme importance in war is to attack the enemy's strategy"

— Sun Tzu, Art of War

In this chapter, we will attack the WLAN infrastructure's core! We will focus on how we can penetrate into the authorized network using various new attack vectors and lure authorized clients to connect to us, as an attacker.

The WLAN infrastructure is what provides wireless services to all the WLAN clients in a system. In this chapter, we will take a look at the various attacks that can be conducted against the infrastructure:

- ◆ Default accounts and credentials on the access point
- ◆ Denial of service attacks
- ◆ Evil twin and access point MAC spoofing
- ◆ Rogue access points

Default accounts and credentials on the access point

WLAN access points are the core building blocks of a wireless infrastructure. Even though they play such an important role, they are sometimes the most neglected in terms of security. In this exercise, we will check whether the default passwords have been changed on the access point or not. Then, we will go on to verify that, even if the passwords have been changed, they are still easy to guess and crack using a dictionary-based attack.

It is important to note that, as we move on to more advanced chapters, it will be assumed that you have gone through the previous chapters and are now familiar with the use of all the tools discussed there. This will allow us to build on that knowledge and try more complicated attacks!

Time for action – cracking default accounts on the access points

Follow these instructions to get started:

1. Let's first connect to our Wireless Lab access point and attempt to navigate to the HTTP management interface. We see that the access point model is **TP-LINK Wireless N Router WR841N**, as shown in the following screenshot:

2. From the manufacturer's website, we find the default password for admin is admin. We try this on the login page and we succeed in logging in. This shows how easy it is to break into accounts with default credentials. We highly encourage you to obtain the router's user manual online. This will allow you to understand what you are dealing with during the penetration test and gives you an insight into other configuration flaws you could check for.

What just happened?

We verified that the default credentials were never changed on this access point, and this could lead to a full network compromise. Also, even if the default credentials are changed, the result should not be something that is easy to guess or run a simple dictionary-based attack on.

Have a go hero – cracking accounts using brute-force attacks

In the previous exercise, change the password to something that is hard to guess or find in a dictionary and see whether you can crack it using a brute-force approach. Limit the length and characters in the password so that you can succeed at some point. One of the most common tools used to crack HTTP authentication is called **Hydra** and is available on Kali.

Denial of service attacks

WLANs are prone to **Denial of Service (DoS)** attacks using various techniques, including but not limited to:

◆ Deauthentication attacks

◆ Disassociation attacks

◆ CTS-RTS attacks

◆ Signal interference or spectrum jamming attacks

In the scope of this book, we will discuss deauthentication attacks on the WLAN infrastructure using the following experiment.

Time for action – deauthentication DoS attack

Follow these instructions to get started:

1. Let's configure the Wireless Lab network to use Open Authentication and no encryption. This will allow us to see the packets using Wireshark easily:

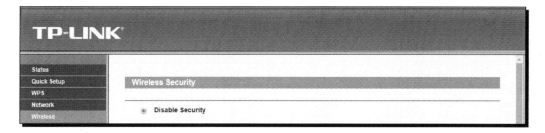

2. Let's connect a Windows client to the access point. We will see the connection in the `airodump-ng` screen:

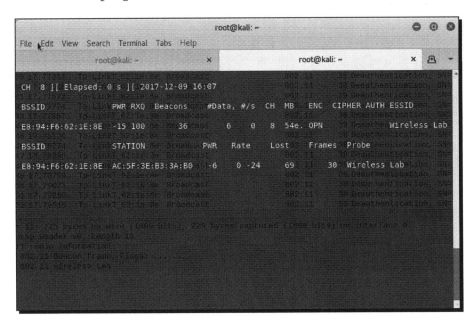

3. Now, on the attacker machine, let's run a directed deauthentication attack against this:

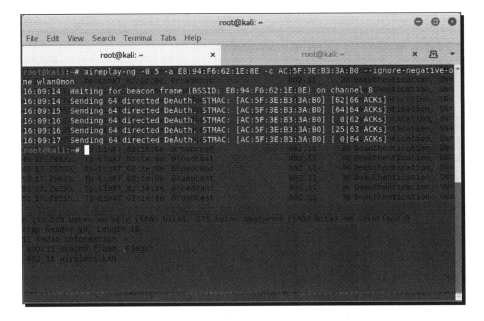

4. Note how the client gets disconnected from the access point completely. We can verify this on the `airodump-ng` screen as well:

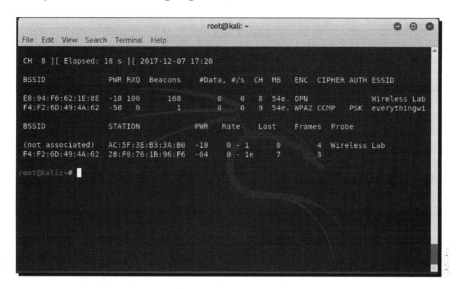

5. If we use Wireshark to see the traffic, you will notice a lot of deauthentication packets that we just sent over the air:

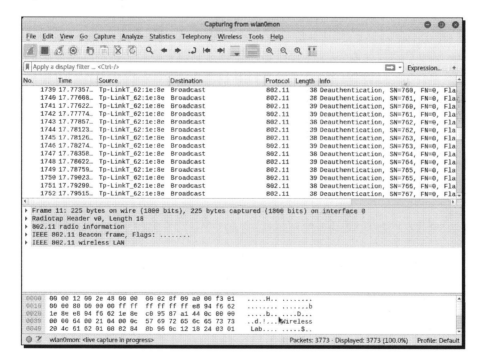

6. We can do the same attack by sending a Broadcast deauthentication packet on behalf of the access point to the entire wireless network. This will have the effect of disconnecting all connected clients:

```
root@kali:~# aireplay-ng -0 5 -a E8:94:F6:62:1E:8E --ignore-negative-one wlan0mon
17:20:53  Waiting for beacon frame (BSSID: E8:94:F6:62:1E:8E) on channel 8
NB: this attack is more effective when targeting
a connected wireless client (-c <client's mac>).
17:20:53  Sending DeAuth to broadcast -- BSSID: [E8:94:F6:62:1E:8E]
17:20:54  Sending DeAuth to broadcast -- BSSID: [E8:94:F6:62:1E:8E]
17:20:54  Sending DeAuth to broadcast -- BSSID: [E8:94:F6:62:1E:8E]
17:20:54  Sending DeAuth to broadcast -- BSSID: [E8:94:F6:62:1E:8E]
17:20:55  Sending DeAuth to broadcast -- BSSID: [E8:94:F6:62:1E:8E]
root@kali:~#
```

What just happened?

We successfully sent deauthentication frames to both the access point and the client. This resulted in them getting disconnected and a full loss of communication between them.

We also sent out Broadcast deauthentication packets, which will ensure that no client in the vicinity can successfully connect to our access point.

It is important to note that, as soon as the client is disconnected, it will try to connect back once again to the access point, and thus the deauthentication attack has to be carried out in a sustainable way to have a full DoS effect.

This is one of the easiest attacks to orchestrate but has the most devastating effect. This can easily be used in the real world to bring a wireless network down on its knees.

Have a go hero – disassociation attacks

Try to check how you can conduct disassociation attacks against the infrastructure using tools available in Kali. Can you do a broadcast disassociation attack?

Evil twin and access point MAC spoofing

One of the most potent attacks on WLAN infrastructures is the **evil twin**. The idea is to basically introduce an attacker-controlled access point in the vicinity of the WLAN network. This access point will advertise the exact same SSID as the authorized WLAN network.

Many wireless users may accidentally connect to this malicious access point, thinking it is part of the authorized network. Once a connection is established, the attacker can orchestrate a man-in-the-middle attack and transparently relay traffic while eavesdropping on the entire communication. We will take a look at how a man-in-the-middle attack is done in a later chapter. In the real world, an attacker would ideally use this attack close to the authorized network so that the user gets confused and accidentally connects to the attacker's network.

An evil twin having the same MAC address as an authorized access point is even more difficult to detect and deter. This is where access point MAC spoofing comes in! In the next experiment, we will take a look at how to create an evil twin, coupled with access point MAC spoofing.

Time for action – evil twin with MAC spoofing

Follow these instructions to get started:

1. Use `airodump-ng` to locate the access point's BSSID and ESSID, which we would like to emulate in the evil twin:

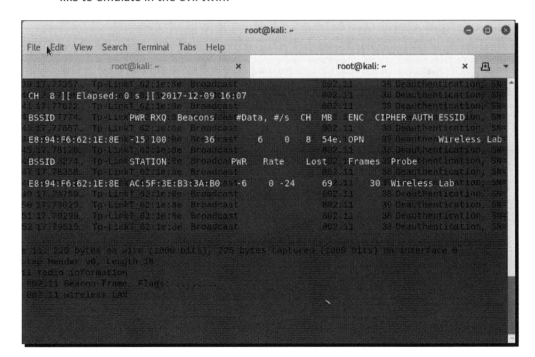

2. Using this information, we create a new access point with the following `airbase-ng` command: `airbase-ng –essid <your chosen ssid> -c <channel> <interface>`. Minor errors may occur with newer releases:

3. This new access point also shows up in the `airodump-ng` screen. It is important to note that you will need to run `airodump-ng` in a new window with the following command:

```
airodump-ng -c <channel> wlan0mon
```

Let's see this new access point:

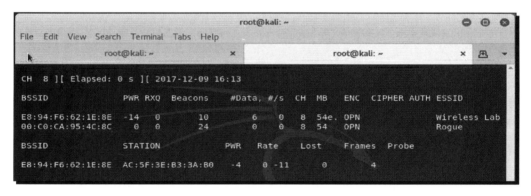

4. What we will do now is spoof the ESSID and MAC address of the access point using the following command:

```
airbase-ng –a <router mac> --essid "Wireless Lab" –c 11 wlan0mon
```

5. Now if we look at through `airodump-ng`, it is almost impossible to differentiate between both visually:

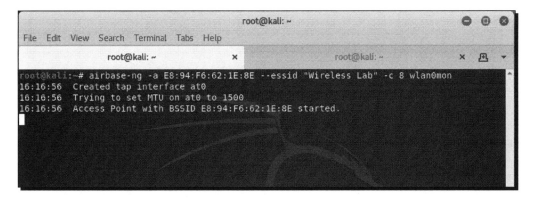

6. Even `airodump-ng` is unable to discern that there are actually two different physical access points on the same channel. This is the most potent form of the evil twin.

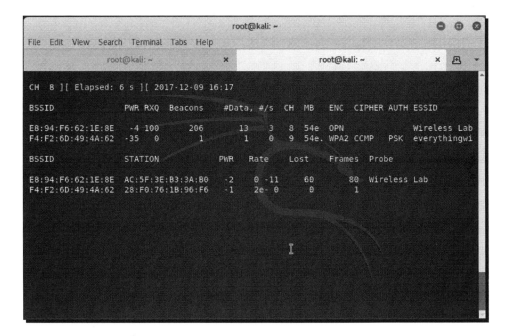

7. Now we send a deauthentication frame to the client, so it disconnects and immediately tries to reconnect:

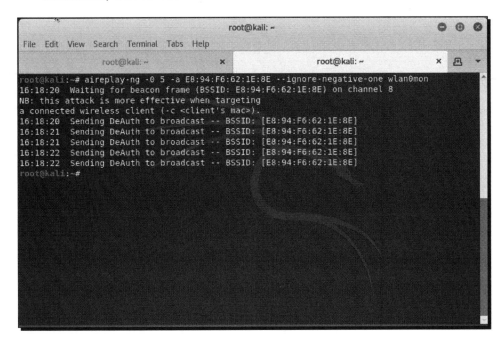

8. As we are closer to this client, our signal strength is higher, and it connects to our evil twin access point. As shown by the following airbase-ng output:

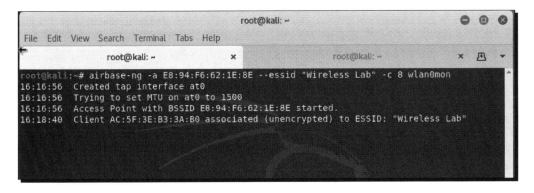

What just happened?

We created an evil twin for the authorized network and used a deauthentication attack to have the legitimate client connect back to us, instead of the authorized network access point.

It is important to note that, in the case of the authorized access point using encryption such as WEP/WPA, it is more difficult to conduct an attack in which traffic eavesdropping is possible. We will take a look at how to break the WEP key with just a client using the Caffe Latte attack in a later chapter.

Have a go hero – evil twin and channel hopping

In the previous exercise, run the evil twin on different channels and observe how the client, once disconnected, hops channels to connect to the access point. What is the deciding factor based on which the client decides which access point to connect to? Is it signal strength? Experiment and validate.

A rogue access point

A **rogue access point** is an unauthorized access point connected to the authorized network. Typically, this access point can be used as a backdoor entry by an attacker, thus enabling him to bypass all security controls on the network. This would mean that the firewalls, intrusion prevention systems, and so on, which guard the border of a network, would be able to do little to stop him from accessing the network.

In the most common case, a rogue access point is set to Open Authentication and no encryption. The rogue access point can be created in the following two ways:

- ◆ Installing an actual physical device on the authorized network as a rogue access point. (This is something I leave as an exercise to you.) Also, more than wireless security, this has to do with breaching the physical security of the authorized network.

- ◆ Creating a rogue access point in software and bridging it with the local authorized Ethernet network. This will allow practically any laptop running on the authorized network to function as a rogue access point. We will look at this in the next experiment.

Time for action – Setting up a rogue access point

Follow these instructions to get started:

1. Let's first bring up our rogue access point using `airbase-ng` and give it the ESSID `Rogue`:

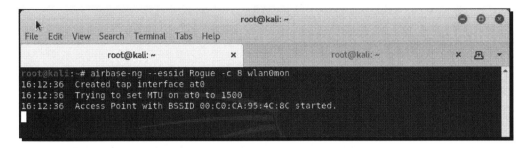

2. We now want to create a bridge between the Ethernet interface, which is part of the authorized network, and our rogue access point interface. To do this, we will first install `bridge-utils` files, create a bridge interface, and name it `Wifi-Bridge`:

```
apt-get install bridge-utils
brctl addbr Wifi-Bridge
```

The following screenshot shows the required commands in action:

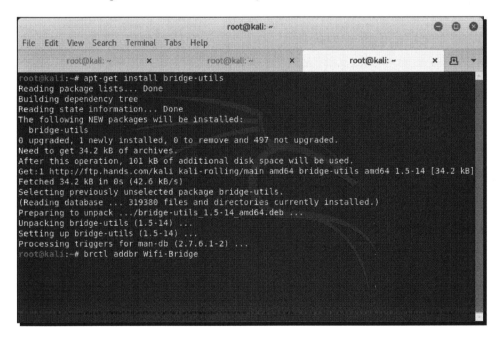

3. We will then add both the Ethernet and the `at0` virtual interface created by `airbase-ng` to this bridge:

```
brctl addif Wifi-Bridge eth0
brctl addif Wifi-Bridge at0
```

The screenshot of the command is as follows:

4. We will then bring up this interfaces to enable the bridge with the following commands:

```
ifconfig eth0 0.0.0.0 up
ifconfig at0 0.0.0.0 up
```

The screenshot of the command is as follows:

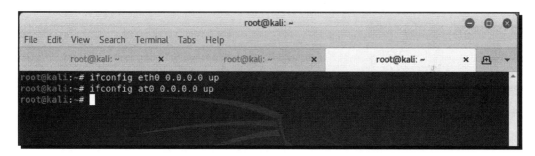

5. We will then enable IP forwarding in the kernel to ensure that packets are forwarded:

```
echo 1 > /proc/sys/net/ipv4/ip_forward
```

The screenshot of the command is as follows:

6. Brilliant! We are done. Now, any wireless client connecting to our rogue access point will have full access to the authorized network using the wireless-to-wired `Wifi-Bridge` we just built. We can verify this by connecting a client to the rogue access point.

7. Then bring the bridge up with:

   ```
   ifconfig Wifi-Bridge up
   ```

8. Notice that it receives an IP address from the DHCP daemon running on the authorized LAN.

9. We can now access any host on the wired network from this wireless client using this rogue access point.

What just happened?

We created a rogue access point and used it to bridge all the authorized network LAN traffic over the wireless network. As you can see, this is a really serious security threat as anyone can break into the wired network using this bridge.

Have a go hero – rogue access point challenge

Check whether you can create a rogue access point that uses WPA/WPA2-based encryption to look more legitimate on the wireless network.

Pop quiz – attacks on the WLAN infrastructure

Q1. What encryption does a rogue access point use in most cases?

   1. None
   2. WEP
   3. WPA
   4. WPA2

Q2. What is the advantage of having the same MAC address as the authorized access point in an evil twin?

1. It makes detecting the evil twin more difficult
2. It forces the client to connect to it
3. It increases the signal strength of the network
4. None of the above

Q3. What do DoS attacks do?

1. They bring down the overall throughput of the network
2. They do not target the clients
3. They can only be done if we know the network WEP/WPA/WPA2 credentials
4. All of the above

Q4. What do rogue access points do and how can they be created?

1. They allow backdoor entry into the authorized network
2. They use WPA2 encryption only
3. They can be created as software-based access points or can be actual devices
4. Both 1 and 3

Summary

In this chapter, we explored different ways to compromise the security of the Wireless LAN infrastructure:

*   Compromising default accounts and credentials on access points
*   Denial of service attacks
*   Evil twins and MAC spoofing
*   Rogue access points in the enterprise network

In the next chapter, we will take a look at different attacks on the Wireless LAN client. Interestingly, most administrators feel that the client has no security problems to worry about. We will see how nothing could be further from the truth.

6
Attacking the Client

"Security is just as strong as the weakest link."

— Famous Quote in Information Security Domain

Most penetration testers seem to give all their attention to the WLAN infrastructure and don't give the wireless client even a fraction of that. However, it is interesting to note that a hacker can gain access to the authorized network by compromising a wireless client as well.

In this chapter, we will shift our focus from the WLAN infrastructure to the wireless client. The client can be either a connected or isolated unassociated client. We will take a look at the various attacks that can be used to target the client.

We will cover the following topics:

- ◆ Honeypot and Misassociation attacks
- ◆ The Caffe Latte attack
- ◆ Deauthentication and disassociation attacks
- ◆ The Hirte attack
- ◆ AP-less WPA-Personal cracking

Honeypot and Misassociation attacks

Normally, when a wireless client such as a laptop is turned on, it will probe for networks it has previously connected to. These networks are stored in a list called the **Preferred Network List** (**PNL**) on Windows-based systems. Also, along with this list, the wireless client will display any networks available in its range.

A hacker may do one or more of the following things:

♦ Silently monitor the probes and bring up a fake access point with the same ESSID the client is searching for. This will cause the client to connect to the hacker machine, thinking it is the legitimate network.

♦ Create fake access points with the same ESSID as neighboring ones to persuade the user to connect to him. Such attacks are very easy to conduct in coffee shops and airports where a user might be looking to connect to a Wi-Fi connection.

♦ Use recorded information to learn about the victim's movements and habits, as we show in detail in a later chapter.

These attacks are called **Honeypot attacks**, because the hacker's access point is misassociated with the legitimate one.

In the next exercise, we will carry out both these attacks in our lab.

Time for action – orchestrating a Misassociation attack

Follow these instructions to get started:

1. In the previous labs, we used a client that had connected to the Wireless Lab access point. Let's switch on the client but not the actual Wireless Lab access point. Let's now run airodump-ng wlan0mon and check the output. You will very soon find the client to be in the not associated mode and probing for Wireless Lab and other SSIDs in its stored profile:

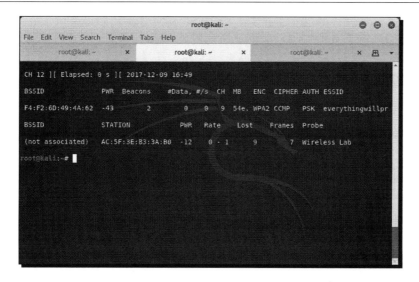

2. To understand what is happening, let's run Wireshark and start sniffing on
    the `wlan0mon` interface. As expected, you might see a lot of packets that are
    not relevant to our analysis. Apply a Wireshark filter to only display Probe
    Request packets from the client MAC you are using. The filter should be `wlan.`
    `addr==<your mac> && wlan.fc.subtype==0x04`):

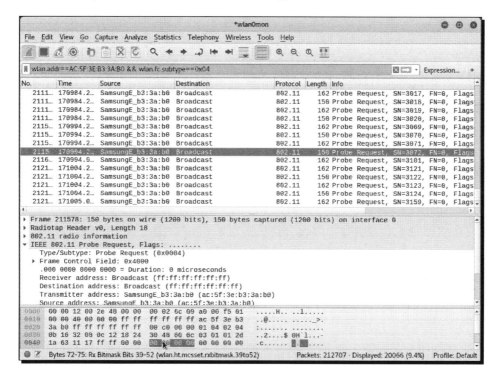

3. You should now see Probe Request packets only from the client for the previously identified SSIDs.

4. Let's now start a fake access point for the network `Wireless Lab` on the hacker machine using the following command:

```
airbase-ng -a <MAC> --essid "Wireless Lab" -c <channel> wlan0mon
```

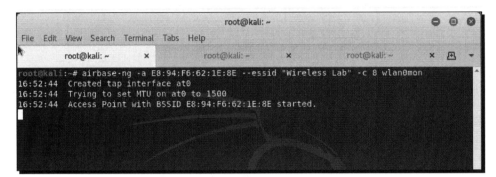

5. Within a minute or so, the client should connect to us automatically. This shows how easy it is to have unassociated clients:

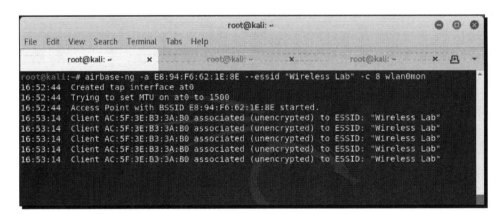

6. Now, we will try it in competition with another router. We will create a fake access point `Wireless Lab` in the presence of the legitimate one. Let's turn our access point on to ensure that `Wireless Lab` is available to the client. For this experiment, we have set the access point channel to `13`. Let the client connect to the access point. We can verify this from `airodump-ng`, as shown in the following screenshot:

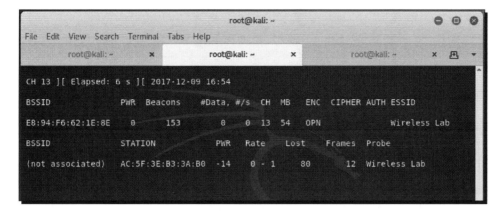

7. Now, let's bring up our fake access point with the SSID `Wireless Lab`:

8. Notice that the client is still connected to `Wireless Lab`, the legitimate access point:

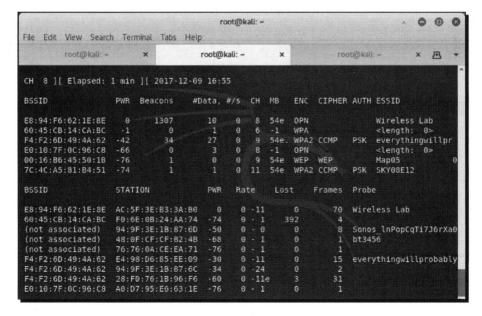

9. We will now send broadcast deauthentication messages to the client on behalf of the legitimate access point to break their connection:

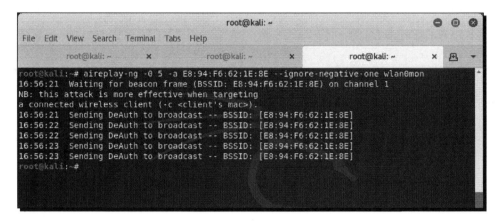

Assuming the signal strength of our fake access point Wireless Lab is stronger than the legitimate one to the client, it connects to our fake access point instead of the legitimate access point.

We can verify this by looking at the airbase-ng output to see the new association of the client with our fake access point:

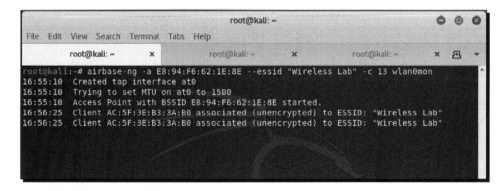

What just happened?

We just created a Honeypot using the probed list from the client and using the same ESSID as that of neighboring access points. In the first case, the client automatically connected to us, as it was searching for the network. In the latter case, as we were closer to the client than the real access point, our signal strength was higher, and the client connected to us.

Have a go hero – forcing a client to connect to the Honeypot

In the previous exercise, what do we do if the client does not automatically connect to us? We would have to send a deauthentication packet to break the legitimate client-access point connection and then, if our signal strength is higher, the client will connect to our spoofed access point. Try this out by connecting a client to a legitimate access point, and then force them to connect to your Honeypot.

The Caffe Latte attack

In the Honeypot attack, we noticed that clients will continuously probe for SSIDs they have connected to previously. If the client had connected to an access point using WEP, operating systems such as Windows cache and store the WEP key. The next time the client connects to the same access point, the Windows wireless configuration manager automatically uses the stored key.

The **Caffe Latte attack** was invented by Vivek, one of the authors of this book, and was demonstrated in Toorcon 9, San Diego, USA. The Caffe Latte attack is a WEP attack that allows a hacker to retrieve the WEP key of the authorized network, using just the client. The attack does not require the client to be anywhere close to the authorized WEP network. It can crack the WEP key using just the isolated client.

In the next exercise, we will retrieve the WEP key of a network from a client using the Caffe Latte attack.

Time for action – conducting the Caffe Latte attack

Follow these instructions to get started:

1. Let's first set up our legitimate access point with WEP for the network `Wireless Lab` with the `ABCDEFABCDEFABCDEF12` key in hex:

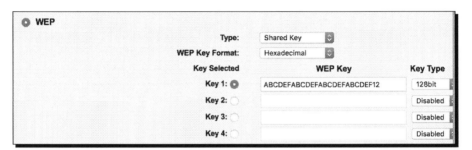

Let's connect our client to it and verify that the connection is successful using `airodump-ng`, as shown in the following screenshot:

2. Let's unplug the access point and ensure that the client is in the unassociated stage and searches for the WEP network `Wireless Lab`.

3. Now, we use `airbase-ng` to bring up an access point with `Wireless Lab` as the SSID, with the parameters `airbase-ng -a <AP MAC> --essid <AP SSID> -L -W 1 -c <channel> wlan0mon`, as shown here:

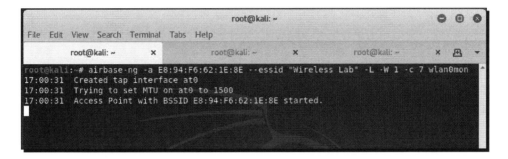

4. As soon as the client connects to this access point, `airbase-ng` starts the Caffe Latte attack, as shown here:

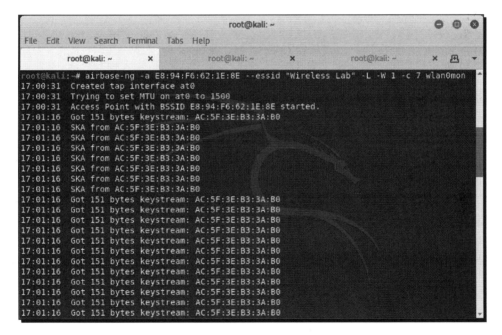

5. We now start `airodump-ng` to collect the data packets from this access point only, as we did before in the WEP cracking scenario `airodump-ng wlan0mon -c <AP channel> --essid <AP SSID> -w <prefix>`:

6. We also start `aircrack-ng` as in the WEP-cracking exercise we did before to begin the cracking process. The command line will be `aircrack-ng filename`, where the filename is the name of the file created by `airodump-ng`.

What just happened?

We were successful in retrieving the WEP key from just the wireless client without requiring an actual access point to be used or present in the vicinity. This is the power of the Caffe Latte attack.

In basic terms, a WEP access point doesn't need to prove to a client that it knows the WEP key in order to receive encrypted traffic. The first piece of traffic that will always be sent to a router upon connecting to a new network will be an ARP request to ask for an IP.

The attack works by bit flipping and replaying ARP packets sent by the wireless client post association with the fake access point created by us. These bit flipped ARP request packets cause more ARP response packets to be sent by the wireless client.

Bit-flipping takes an encrypted value and alters it to create a different encrypted value. In this circumstance, we can take an encrypted ARP request and create an ARP response with a high degree of accuracy. Once we send back a valid ARP response, we can replay this value over and over again to generate the traffic we need to decrypt the WEP key.

Note that all these packets are encrypted using the WEP key stored on the client. Once we are able to gather a large number of these data packets, `aircrack-ng` is able to recover the WEP key easily.

Have a go hero – practise makes you perfect!

Try changing the WEP key and repeat the attack. This is a difficult attack and requires some practice to orchestrate successfully. It would also be a good idea to use Wireshark and examine the traffic on the wireless network.

Deauthentication and disassociation attacks

We have seen deauthentication attacks in previous chapters as well in the context of the access point. In this chapter, we will explore this attack in the context of the client.

In the next lab, we will send deauthentication packets to just the client and break an established connection between the access point and the client.

Time for action – deauthenticating the client

Follow these instructions to get started:

1. Let's first bring our access point `Wireless Lab` online again. Let's keep it running on WEP to prove that, even with encryption enabled, it is possible to attack the access point and client connection. Let's verify that the access point is up using `airodump-ng`:

2. Let's connect our client to this access point and verify it with `airodump-ng`:

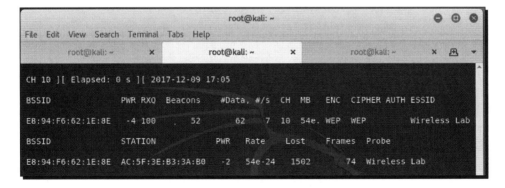

3. We will now run `aireplay-ng` to target the access point connection:

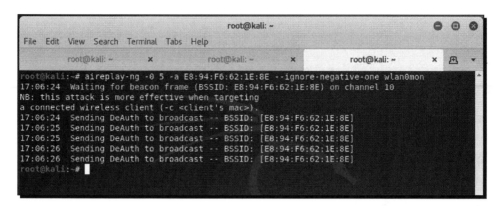

4. The client gets disconnected and tries to reconnect to the access point. We can verify this using Wireshark, just as we did earlier:

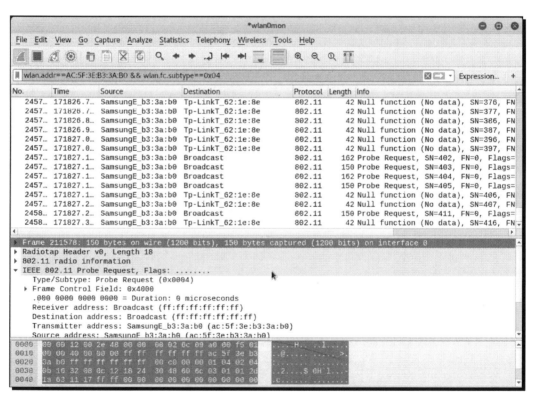

5. We have now seen that, even in the presence of WEP encryption, it is possible to deauthenticate a client and disconnect it. The same is valid even in the presence of WPA/WPA2. Let's now set our access point to WPA encryption and verify it:

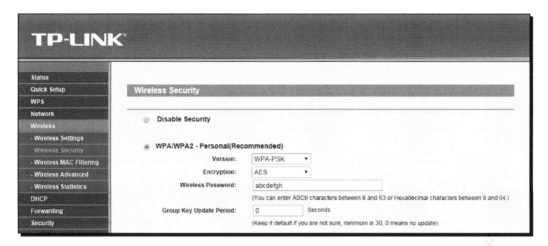

6. Let's connect our client to the access point and ensure that it is connected:

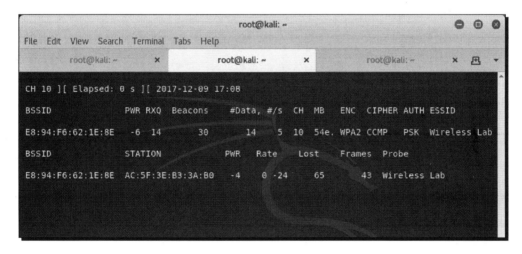

7. Let's now run `aireplay-ng` to disconnect the client from the access point:

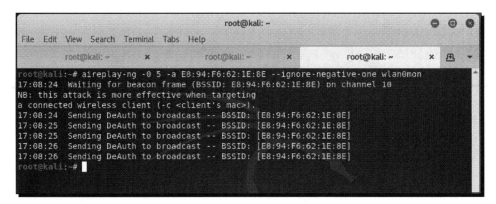

What just happened?

We just learnt how to disconnect a wireless client selectively from an access point using deauthentication frames even in the presence of encryption schemas such as WEP/WPA/WPA2. This was done by sending a deauthentication packet to just the access point-client pair, instead of sending a broadcast deauthentication to the entire network.

Have a go hero – dissociation attack on the client

In the previous exercise, we used a deauthentication attack to break the connection. Try using a disassociation packet to break the established connection between a client and an access point.

The Hirte attack

We've already seen how to conduct the Caffe Latte attack. The Hirte attack extends the Caffe Latte attack using fragmentation techniques and allows almost any packet to be used.

More information on the Hirte attack is available on the Aircrack-ng website at `http://www.aircrack-ng.org/doku.php?id=hirte`.

We will now use `aircrack-ng` to conduct a Hirte attack on the same client.

Time for action – cracking WEP with the Hirte attack

Follow these instructions to get started:

1. Create a WEP access point exactly as in the Caffe Latte attack using the `airbase-ng` tool. The only additional option is the `-N` option instead of the `-L` option to launch the Hirte attack:

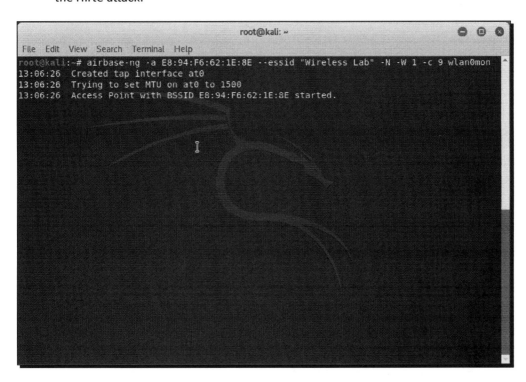

2. Start `airodump-ng` in a separate window to capture packets for the `Wireless Lab` **Honeypot**:

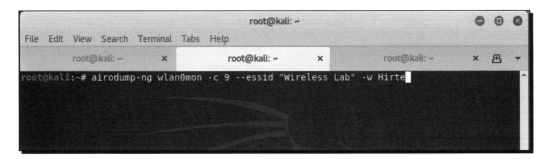

3. Now, `airodump-ng` will start monitoring this network and storing the packets in the `Hirte-01.cap` file:

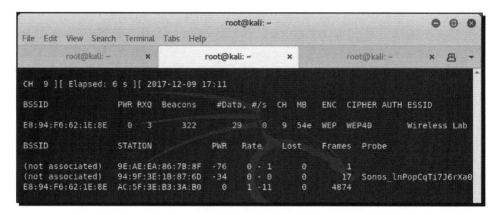

4. Once the roaming client connects to our Honeypot AP, the Hirte attack is automatically launched by `airbase-ng`:

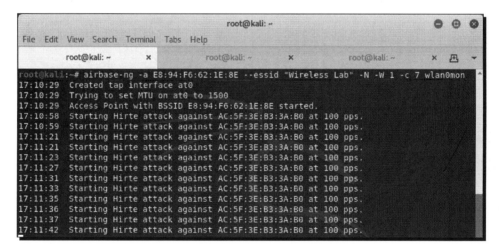

5. We start `aircrack-ng` as in the case of the Caffe Latte attack and eventually, the key will be cracked.

What just happened?

We launched the Hirte attack against a WEP client that was isolated and away from the authorized network. We cracked the key exactly the same way as in the Caffe Latte attack case.

We recommend setting different WEP keys on the client and trying this exercise a couple of times to gain confidence. You may notice many times that you may have to reconnect the client to get it to work.

AP-less WPA-Personal cracking

In *Chapter 4, WLAN Encryption Flaws*, we saw how to crack WPA/WPA2 PSK using `aircrack-ng`. The basic idea was to capture a four-way WPA handshake and then launch a dictionary attack.

The million-dollar question is: would it be possible to crack WPA-Personal with just the client? No, access point!

Let's revisit the WPA cracking exercise to jog our memory:

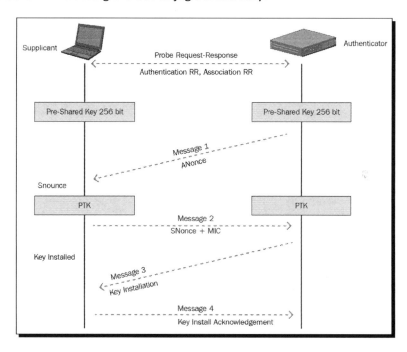

To crack WPA, we need the following four parameters from the four-way handshake—**Authenticator Nounce (ANonce)**, **Supplicant Nounce (SNonce)**, Authenticator MAC, and Supplicant MAC. Now, the interesting thing is that we do not need all of the four packets in the handshake to extract this information. We can get this information with four packets; packets 1 and 2 or just packets 2 and 3.

In order to crack WPA-PSK, we will bring up a WPA-PSK Honeypot and, when the client connects to us, only **Message 1** and **Message 2** will come through. As we do not know the passphrase, we cannot send **Message 3**. However, **Message 1** and **Message 2** contain all the information required to begin the key cracking process:

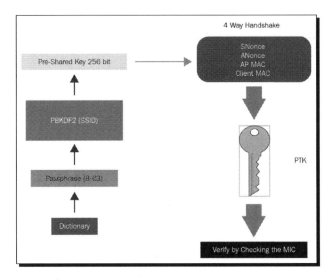

Time for action – AP-less WPA cracking

1. We will set up a WPA-PSK Honeypot with the ESSID `Wireless Lab`. The `-z 2` option creates a WPA-PSK access point, which uses TKIP:

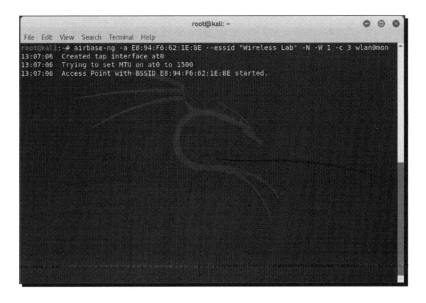

2. Let's also start `airodump-ng` to capture packets from this network:

3. Now, when our roaming client connects to this access point, it starts the handshake but fails to complete it after **Message 2**, as discussed previously; however, the data required to crack the handshake has been captured.

4. We run the `airodump-ng` capture file through `aircrack-ng` with the same dictionary file as before; eventually, the passphrase is cracked as before.

What just happened?

We were able to crack the WPA key with just the client. This was possible because, even with just the first two packets, we have all the information required to launch a dictionary attack on the handshake.

Have a go hero – AP-less WPA cracking

We recommend setting different WEP keys on the client and trying this exercise a couple of times to gain confidence. You may notice many times that you have to reconnect the client to get it to work.

Pop quiz – attacking the client

Q1. What encryption key can the Caffe Latte attack recover?

1. None
2. WEP
3. WPA
4. WPA2

Q2. What would a Honeypot access point typically use?

1. No Encryption, Open Authentication
2. No Encryption, Shared Authentication
3. WEP Encryption, Open Authentication
4. None of the above

Q3. Which one of the following is a DoS Attack?

1. Misassociation attacks
2. Deauthentication attacks
3. Disassociation attacks
4. Both 2 and 3

Q4. What does the Caffe Latte attack require?

1. That the wireless client be in radio range of the access point
2. That the client contains a cached and stored WEP key
3. WEP encryption with at least 128-bit encryption
4. Both 1 and 3

Summary

In this chapter, we learned that even the wireless client is susceptible to attacks. These include the Honeypot and other Misassociation attacks; Caffe Latte attack, to retrieve the key from the wireless client, deauthentication and disassociation attacks causing a Denial of Service, Hirte attack as an alternative to retrieve the WEP key from a roaming client, and, finally, cracking the WPA-Personal passphrase with just the client.

In the next chapter, we will use what we've learned so far to conduct various advanced wireless attacks on both the client and infrastructure side. So, quickly flip the page to the next chapter!

7
Advanced WLAN Attacks

"To know your enemy, you must become your enemy."

− Sun Tzu, Art of War

As a penetration tester, it is important to know the advanced attacks a hacker can do, even if you might not check or demonstrate them during a penetration test. This chapter is dedicated to showing how a hacker can conduct advanced attacks using wireless access as the starting point.

In this chapter, we will take a look at how we can conduct advanced attacks using what we have learned so far. We will primarily focus on the **Man-in-the-Middle (MITM)** attack, which requires a certain amount of skill and practice to conduct successfully. Once we have done this, we will use this MITM attack as a base from which to conduct more sophisticated attacks such as eavesdropping and session hijacking.

In this chapter, we will cover the following topics:

◆ MITM attack

◆ Wireless eavesdropping using MITM

◆ Session hijacking using MITM

A Man-in-the-Middle attack

MITM attacks are probably one of the most potent attacks on a WLAN system. There are different configurations that can be used to conduct the attack. We will use the most common one—the attacker is connected to the internet using a wired LAN and is creating a fake access point on his client card. This access point broadcasts an SSID similar to a local hotspot in the vicinity. A user may accidently get connected to this fake access point (or can be forced to via the higher signal strength theory we discussed in the previous chapters) and may continue to believe that he is connected to the legitimate access point.

The attacker can now transparently forward all the user's traffic over the internet using the bridge he has created between the wired and wireless interfaces.

In the following lab exercise, we will simulate this attack.

Time for action – Man-in-the-Middle attack

Follow these instructions to get started:

1. To create the MITM attack setup, we will first create a soft access point called `mitm` on the hacker laptop using `airbase-ng`. We run the following command:

    ```
    airbase-ng --essid mitm -c 11 wlan0mon
    ```

    The output of the command is as follows:

2. It is important to note that `airbase-ng`, when run, creates an interface `at0` (a tap interface). Think of this as the wired-side interface of our software-based access point `mitm`:

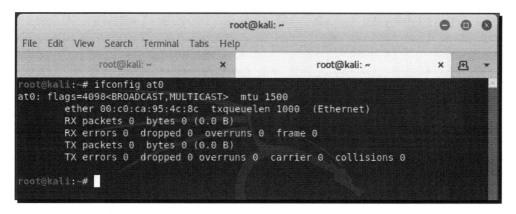

3. Let's now create a bridge on the hacker's laptop, consisting of the wired (eth0) and wireless interface (at0). The succession of commands used for this is as follows:

- `brctl addbr mitm-bridge`
- `brctl addif mitm-bridge eth0`
- `brctl addif mitm-bridge at0`
- `ifconfig eth0 0.0.0.0 up`
- `ifconfig at0 0.0.0.0 up`

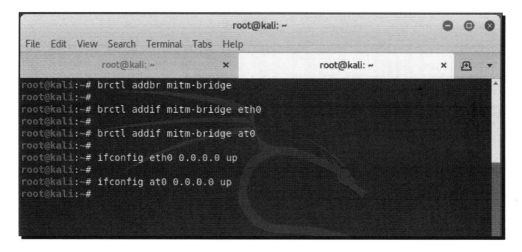

4. We can assign an IP address to this bridge and check the connectivity with the gateway. Please note that we can do this using DHCP as well. We can assign an IP address to the bridge interface with the following command:

```
ifconfig mitm-bridge 192.168.0.199 up
```

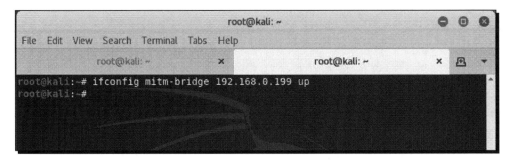

We can then try pinging the gateway `192.168.0.1` to ensure that we are connected to the rest of the network.

5. Let's now turn on IP forwarding in the kernel, so that routing and packet forwarding can happen correctly, using the following command:

```
echo 1 > /proc/sys/net/ipv4/ip_forward
```

The output of the command is as follows:

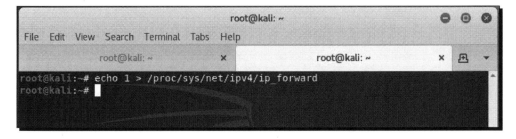

6. Now let's connect a wireless client to our access point `mitm`. It will automatically get an IP address over DHCP (the server running on the wired-side gateway). The client machine in this case receives the IP address `192.168.0.197`. We can ping the wired-side gateway `192.168.0.1` to verify connectivity:

```
C:\Users\vivek\AppData\Local\msf32>ipconfig

Windows IP Configuration

Wireless LAN adapter Wireless Network Connection:

   Connection-specific DNS Suffix   . :
   Link-local IPv6 Address . . . . . : fe80::693d:fad9:1424:c019%11
   IPv4 Address. . . . . . . . . . . : 192.168.0.197
   Subnet Mask . . . . . . . . . . . : 255.255.255.0
   Default Gateway . . . . . . . . . : 192.168.0.1
```

7. We can see that the host responds to the `ping` requests, as shown here:

```
C:\Users\vivek\AppData\Local\msf32>ping 192.168.0.1

Pinging 192.168.0.1 with 32 bytes of data:
Reply from 192.168.0.1: bytes=32 time=11ms TTL=64
Reply from 192.168.0.1: bytes=32 time=6ms TTL=64
Reply from 192.168.0.1: bytes=32 time=18ms TTL=64
Reply from 192.168.0.1: bytes=32 time=5ms TTL=64

Ping statistics for 192.168.0.1:
    Packets: Sent = 4, Received = 4, Lost = 0 (0% loss),
Approximate round trip times in milli-seconds:
    Minimum = 5ms, Maximum = 18ms, Average = 10ms
```

8. We can also verify that the client is connected by looking at the `airbase-ng` terminal on the hacker's machine:

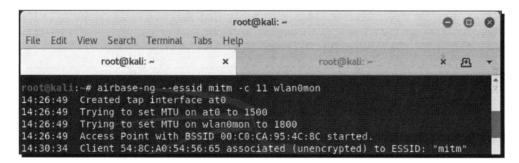

9. It is interesting to note here that, because all the traffic is being relayed from the wireless interface to the wired-side, we have full control over the traffic. We can verify this by starting Wireshark and sniffing on the `at0` interface:

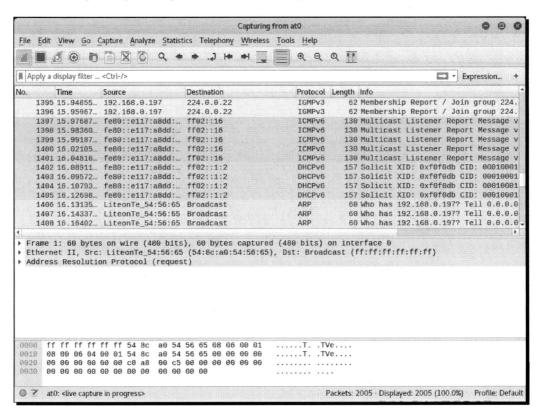

10. Let's now ping the gateway `192.168.0.1` from the client machine. We can see the packets in Wireshark (apply a display filter for ICMP), even though the packets are not destined for us. This is the power of MITM attacks:

```
File  Edit  View  Go  Capture  Analyze  Statistics  Telephony  Wireless  Tools  Help

icmp                                                                    Expression...  +

No.      Time        Source          Destination       Protocol  Length  Info
    122 0.616657..  10.0.2.15       192.168.0.1        ICMP       100  Echo (ping) request  id=0x0653, seq
    123 0.617602..  192.168.0.1     10.0.2.15          ICMP       100  Echo (ping) reply    id=0x0653, seq
    173 1.617627..  10.0.2.15       192.168.0.1        ICMP       100  Echo (ping) request  id=0x0653, seq
    174 1.618602..  192.168.0.1     10.0.2.15          ICMP       100  Echo (ping) reply    id=0x0653, seq
    216 2.619516..  10.0.2.15       192.168.0.1        ICMP       100  Echo (ping) request  id=0x0653, seq
    217 2.620474..  192.168.0.1     10.0.2.15          ICMP       100  Echo (ping) reply    id=0x0653, seq
    284 3.620862..  10.0.2.15       192.168.0.1        ICMP       100  Echo (ping) request  id=0x0653, seq
    285 3.621875..  192.168.0.1     10.0.2.15          ICMP       100  Echo (ping) reply    id=0x0653, seq
    343 4.621241..  10.0.2.15       192.168.0.1        ICMP       100  Echo (ping) request  id=0x0653, seq
    344 4.622196..  192.168.0.1     10.0.2.15          ICMP       100  Echo (ping) reply    id=0x0653, seq
    397 5.622358..  10.0.2.15       192.168.0.1        ICMP       100  Echo (ping) request  id=0x0653, seq
    398 5.623318..  192.168.0.1     10.0.2.15          ICMP       100  Echo (ping) reply    id=0x0653, seq
    456 6.623511..  10.0.2.15       192.168.0.1        ICMP       100  Echo (ping) request  id=0x0653, seq
    457 6.624457..  192.168.0.1     10.0.2.15          ICMP       100  Echo (ping) reply    id=0x0653, seq

▶ Frame 122: 100 bytes on wire (800 bits), 100 bytes captured (800 bits) on interface 0
▶ Linux cooked capture
▶ Internet Protocol Version 4, Src: 10.0.2.15, Dst: 192.168.0.1
▶ Internet Control Message Protocol
```

What just happened?

We successfully created the setup for a wireless MITM attack. We did this by creating a fake access point and bridging it with our Ethernet interface. This ensured that any wireless client connecting to the fake access point will perceive that it is connected to the internet via the wired LAN.

Have a go hero – MITM over pure wireless

In the previous exercise, we bridged the wireless interface with a wired one. As we noted earlier, this is one of the possible connection architectures for an MITM. There are other combinations possible as well. An interesting one would be to have two wireless interfaces, one that creates the fake access point and the other interface that is connected to the authorized access point. Both these interfaces are bridged. So, when a wireless client connects to our fake access point, it gets connected to the authorized access point through the attacker's machine.

Please note that this configuration would require the use of two wireless cards on the attacker's laptop.

Check whether you can conduct this attack using the in-built card on your laptop along with the external one—bear in mind, you may not have the injection drivers required for this activity. This should be a good challenge!

Wireless eavesdropping using MITM

In the previous lab, we learned how to create a setup for MITM. Now, we will take a look at how to do wireless eavesdropping with this setup.

The whole lab revolves around the principle that all the victim's traffic is now routed through the attacker's computer. Thus, the attacker can eavesdrop on all the traffic sent to and from the victim's machine wirelessly.

Time for action – wireless eavesdropping

Follow these instructions to get started:

1. Replicate the entire setup as in the previous lab. Fire up Wireshark. Interestingly, even the MITM-bridge shows up. This interface would allow us to peer into the bridge traffic, if we wanted to:

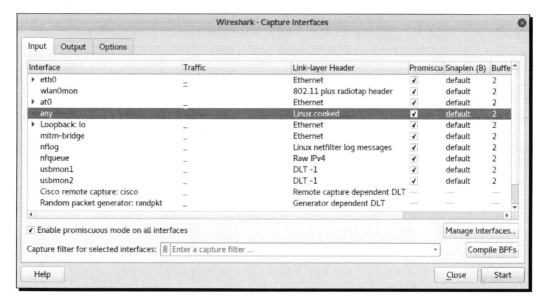

2. Start sniffing on the `at0` interface so that we can monitor all traffic sent and received by the wireless client. On the wireless client, open up any web page. In my case, the wireless access point is also connected to LAN and I will open it up by using the address `http://192.168.0.1`:

3. Sign in with your password and enter the management interface.

4. In Wireshark, we should be seeing a lot of activity:

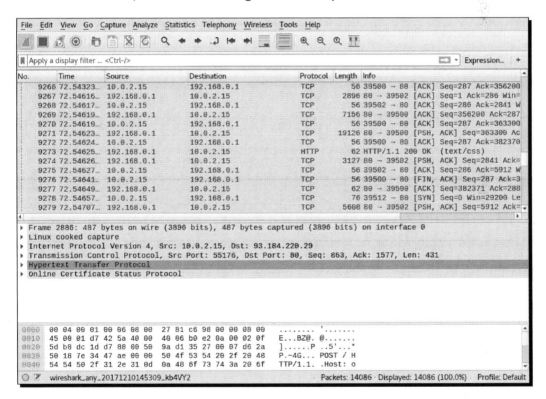

5. Set a filter for HTTP to see only the web traffic:

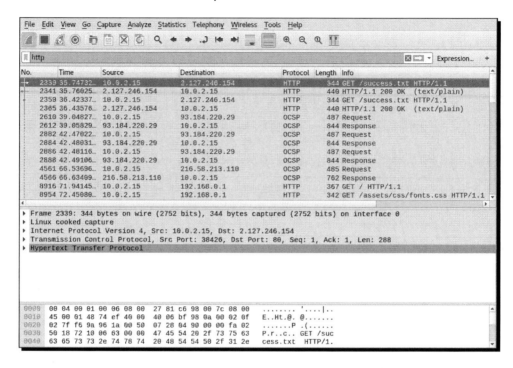

6. We can easily locate the HTTP post request that was used to send the password to the wireless access point:

What just happened?

The MITM setup we created now allows us to eavesdrop on the victim's wireless traffic without the victim knowing. This is possible because, in an MITM, all the traffic is relayed via the attacker's machine. Thus, all of the victim's unencrypted traffic is available for eavesdropping for the attacker.

Session hijacking over wireless

One of the other interesting attacks we can build on top of MITM is application session hijacking. During an MITM attack, the victim's packets are sent to the attacker. It is now the attacker's responsibility to relay this to the legitimate destination and relay the responses from the destination to the victim. An interesting thing to note is that, during this process, the attacker can modify the data in the packets (if unencrypted and unprotected from tampering). This means he can modify, mangle, and even silently drop packets.

In this next example, we will take a look at DNS hijacking over wireless using the MITM setup. Then, using DNS hijacking, we will hijack the browser session to `https://www.google.com`.

Time for action – session hijacking over wireless

1. Set up the test exactly as in the MITM attack lab. On the victim, let's fire up the browser and type in `https://www.google.com`. Let's use Wireshark to monitor this traffic. Your screen should resemble the following:

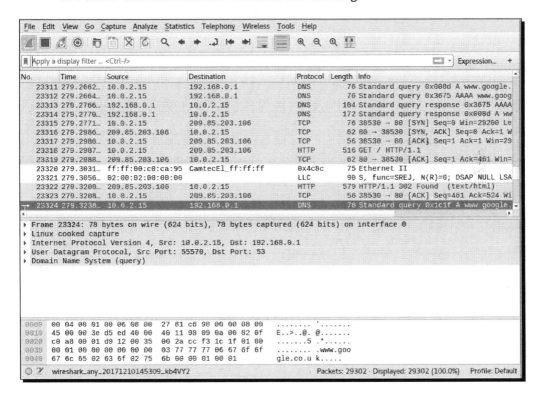

2. Apply a Wireshark filter for DNS and, as we can see, the victim is making DNS requests for `https://www.google.com`:

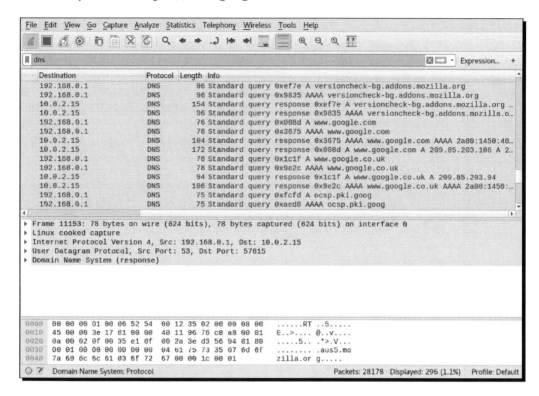

3. In order to hijack the browser session, we will need to send fake DNS responses that will resolve the IP address of `https://www.google.com` to the hacker machine's IP address `192.168.0.199`. The tool that we will use for this is called `dnsspoof` and the syntax is as follows:

```
dnsspoof -i mitm-bridge
```

The output of the command is as follows:

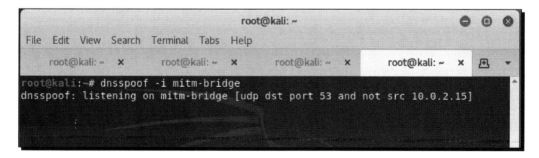

4. Refresh the browser windows and now, as we can see through Wireshark, as soon as the victim makes a DNS request for any host (including `https://www.google.com`), `dnsspoof` replies back.

5. On the victim's machine, we see an error that says **Unable to connect**. This is because we made the IP address for `https://www.google.com` as `192.168.0.199`, which is the hacker machine's IP, but there is no service listening on port `80`:

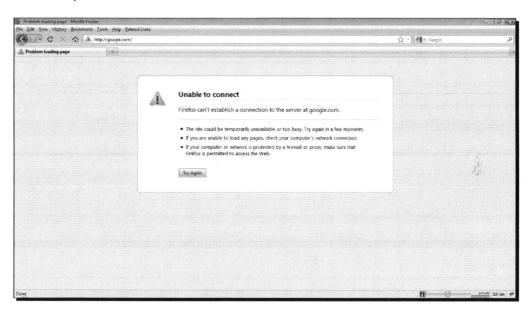

6. Let's run Apache on Kali using the following command:

```
apachet2ctl start
```

The output of the command is as follows:

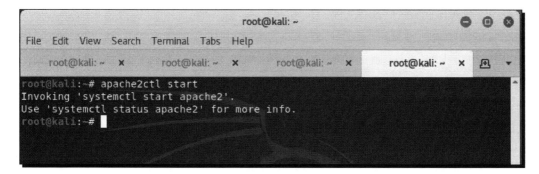

7. Now, once we refresh the browser on the victim, we are greeted with the **It Works!** default page of Apache:

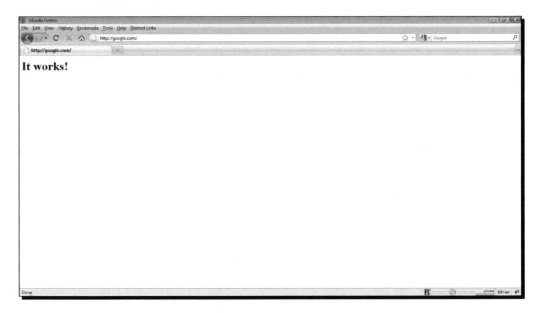

8. This demonstration shows how it is possible to intercept data and send spoofed responses to hijack sessions on the victim.

What just happened?

We did an application hijacking attack using a wireless MITM as the base. So, what happened behind the scenes? The MITM setup ensured that we were able to see all the packets sent by the victim. As soon as we saw a DNS request packet coming from the victim, the `dnsspoof` program running on the attacker's laptop sent a DNS response to the victim with the attacker machine's IP address that of `https://www.google.com`. The victim's laptop accepted this response and the browser sent an HTTP request to the attacker's IP address on port `80`.

In the first part of the experiment, there was no listening process on port 80 of the attacker's machine and thus, Firefox responded with an error. Then, once we started the Apache server on the attacker's machine on port 80 (the default port), the browser's request received a response from the attacker's machine with the default **It Works!** page.

This lab shows us that, once we have full control of the lower layers (Layer 2 in this case), it is easy to hijack applications running on higher layers such as DNS clients and web browsers.

Have a go hero – application hijacking challenge

The next step in session hijacking using a wireless MITM will be to modify the data being transmitted by the client. Explore software available on Kali called **Ettercap**. This will help you create search and replace filters for network traffic.

In this challenge, write a simple filter to replace all occurrences of security in the network traffic to insecurity. Try searching Google for security and check whether the results show up for insecurity instead.

Finding security configurations on the client

In previous chapters, we have seen how to create Honeypots for open access points, WEP-protected and WPA, but, when we are in the field and see probe requests from the client, how do we know which network the probed SSID belongs to?

Though this seems tricky at first, the solution to this problem is simple. We need to create access points advertising the same SSID but with different security configurations simultaneously. When a roaming client searches for a network, it will automatically connect to one of these access points based on the network configuration stored on it.

So, let the games begin!

Time for action – deauthentication attack on the client

We will assume that the wireless client has a network `Wireless Lab` configured on it, and it actively sends probe requests for this network, when it is not connected to any access point. In order to find the security configuration of this network, we will need to create multiple access points. For our discussion, we will assume that the client profile is an open network, WEP protected, WPA-PSK, or WPA2-PSK. This means we will have to create four access points:

1. To do this, we will first create four virtual interfaces—wlan0mon to wlan0mon3, using the `iw wlan0 interface add wlan0mon type monitor` command multiple times adding 1 to the end of the monitor name each time:

```
root@kali:~# iw wlan0 interface add wlan0mon type monitor
root@kali:~#
root@kali:~# iw wlan0 interface add wlan0mon1 type monitor
root@kali:~#
root@kali:~# iw wlan0 interface add wlan0mon2 type monitor
root@kali:~#
root@kali:~# iw wlan0 interface add wlan0mon3 type monitor
root@kali:~#
```

2. You can view all these newly created interfaces using the `iwconfig` command:

```
root@kali:~# iwconfig
wlan0mon   IEEE 802.11  Mode:Monitor  Tx-Power=20 dBm
           Retry short  long limit:2  RTS thr:off   Fragment thr:off
           Power Management:off

wlan0mon3  IEEE 802.11  Mode:Monitor  Tx-Power=20 dBm
           Retry short  long limit:2  RTS thr:off   Fragment thr:off
           Power Management:off

wlan0mon1  IEEE 802.11  Mode:Monitor  Tx-Power=20 dBm
           Retry short  long limit:2  RTS thr:off   Fragment thr:off
           Power Management:off

wlan0mon2  IEEE 802.11  Mode:Monitor  Tx-Power=20 dBm
           Retry short  long limit:2  RTS thr:off   Fragment thr:off
           Power Management:off

lo         no wireless extensions.

eth0       no wireless extensions.

wlan0      IEEE 802.11  ESSID:off/any
           Mode:Managed  Access Point: Not-Associated   Tx-Power=20 dBm
           Retry short  long limit:2  RTS thr:off   Fragment thr:off
           Encryption key:off
           Power Management:off

root@kali:~#
```

3. Now we will create the open AP on `wlan0mon`:

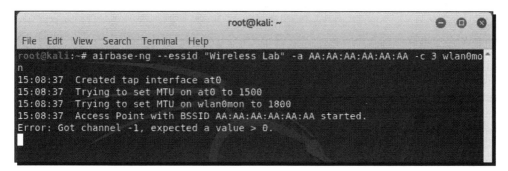

4. Let's create the WEP protected AP on `wlan0mon1`:

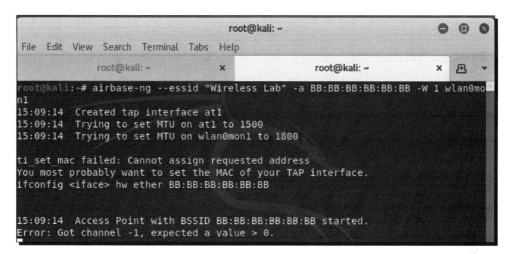

5. The WPA-PSK AP will be on `wlan0mon2`:

6. WPA2-PSK AP will be on `wlan0mon3`:

7. We can run `airodump-ng` on the same channel to ensure that all four access points are up and running, as shown in the following screenshot:

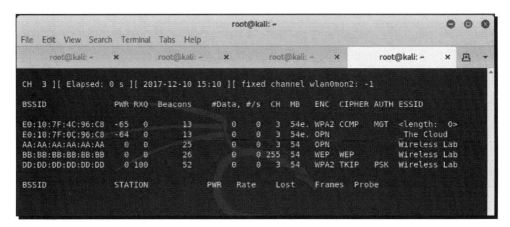

8. Now let's switch the Wi-Fi on the roaming client. Depending on which `Wireless Lab` network you connected it to previously, it will connect to that security configuration. In my case, it connects to the WPA-PSK network, as shown in the following screenshot:

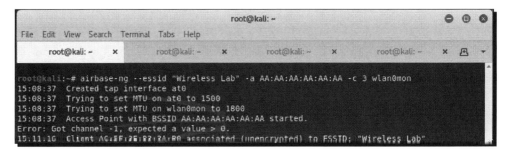

What just happened?

We created multiple Honeypots with the same SSID but different security configurations. Depending on which configuration the client had stored for the `Wireless Lab` network, it connected to the appropriate one.

This technique can come in handy as, if you are doing a penetration test, you won't know which security configurations the client has on its laptop. This allows you to find the appropriate one by setting a bait for the client. This technique is also called **WiFishing**.

Have a go hero – baiting clients

Create different security configurations on the client for the same SSID, and check whether your set of Honeypots is able to detect them.

It is important to note that many Wi-Fi clients might not actively probe for networks they have stored in their profile. It might not be possible to detect these networks using the technique we discussed here.

Pop quiz – advanced WLAN attacks

Q1. In an MITM attack, who is in the middle?

1. The access point
2. The attacker
3. The victim
4. None of the above

Q2. `dnsspoof`:

1. Spoofs DNS requests
2. Spoofs DNS responses
3. Needs to run on the DNS server
4. Needs to run on the access point

Q3. A wireless MITM attack can be orchestrated:

1. On all wireless clients at the same time
2. Only one channel at a time
3. On any SSID
4. Both 2 and 3

Q4. Which is the interface closest to the victim in our MITM setup?

1. at0
2. eth0
3. br0
4. en0

Summary

In this chapter, we learned how to conduct advanced attacks using wireless as the base. We created a setup for an MITM attack over wireless and then used it to eavesdrop on the victim's traffic. We then used the same setup to hijack the application layer of the victim (web traffic, to be specific) using a DNS poisoning attack.

In the next chapter, we will learn how to conduct a wireless penetration test right from the planning, discovery, and attack to the reporting stage. We will also touch upon the best practices to secure WLANs.

8

KRACK Attacks

"Disregard mountains. Acquire empires"

— Hannibal (probably)

This chapter discusses the recently identified KRACK vulnerabilities and explores the current state of the tools that enable the identification of vulnerable devices. This chapter is a deep dive into the inner workings of the WPA2 handshake and is recommended for advanced readers.

KRACK attack overview

KRACK stands for **Key Reinstallation AttaCKs**. It's a tranche of vulnerabilities publicly disclosed in October 2017 by a team from KU Leuven. The attack is the exploitation of a fundamental flaw in the WPA2 handshake, allowing resending of a stage of the handshake in order to overwrite cryptographic data. This chapter will cover the attack at a theoretical level and provide some guidance on the successful identification and exploitation of this vulnerability.

Let's look at the WPA2 handshake, the standard for which can be found in the IEEE 802.11 standards, accessible here: `http://ieeexplore.ieee.org/document/7792308/`. For this explanation we are starting post-association and authentication stage as the vulnerability is not affected by those.

The **Pairwise Transient Key (PTK)** used for encryption is made up of five attributes:

- A shared secret key known as the Pairwise Master Key (PMK)
- A nonce value created by the access point (ANonce)
- A nonce value created by the user station (SNonce)
- The access point MAC address (APMAC)
- The user station MAC address (STAMAC)

Throughout the process, **Message Identification Codes (MIC)** are used to provide a level of integrity and security. While these are integral to the process, they are not used in the resulting cryptographic data. Here's a representation:

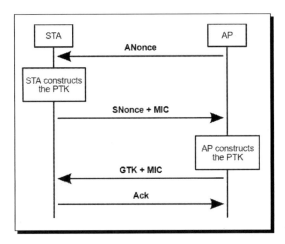

At this time, as a result of the initial authentication and association process, both the user station and the access point have the PMK, the access point MAC address, and the user station MAC address. In addition, each stage will have a Key Replay Counter keeping track of the order of packets; this will come into play later:

1. **Stage 1**: The access point transmits the **ANonce** value to the user station, which provides the user station with everything it needs to generate the PTK. The user station creates the PTK and now holds the key it will use for encryption.

2. **Stage 2**: The user station sends back its own nonce value along with a MIC. The access point now holds everything that it needs to create the PTK. The access point creates the PTK and is in the same state as the user station.

3. **Stage 3**: The access point creates and sends the **Group Temporal Key (GTK)** to the user, which enables the reading of non-directed traffic such as multicast/broadcast traffic.

4. **Stage 4**: The user station returns an acknowledged statement.

Following the four-stage handshake, the user station can now send encrypted data to the access point and have it accepted. At this point, the negotiation phase is complete and the user station is free to use the network.

What just happened?

We discussed the four-stage handshake in preparation for the explanation of the KRACK attacks. This should be a revisit at this stage, but it is important to cover the basics before launching into the technical nitty-gritty of the exploit.

The four-way handshake KRACK attack

Keeping in mind what we just discussed, you may now be surprised to find that this process is vulnerable to attack! However, the issue is not the core concept, but the practical implementation of the standard. As with most technical standards, sacrifices were made to the security of the solution in order to make it user-friendly. In specific, the sacrifice that was made to make the solution usable was making certain stages in the handshake replayable in the event of a missed message.

While this is not a huge issue for most of the process, Stage 3 is replayable and can have a dramatic effect on the security of the overall solution. By placing themselves in a **Man-in-the-Middle (MITM)** position during the authentication process, an attacker can block the correctly negotiated PTK and install their own in certain circumstances. The Key Replay Counter and associated nonce values are reset when a key is negotiated. So by blocking certain packets, an MITM attacker can predict what counter and nonce values are going to be by forcing a key reinstall. This will enable future attackers to perform malicious actions such as decryption, spoofing, and packet replay.

However, in deference to how the security industry operates, researchers have wisely only released **Proof of Concept (PoC)** scripts showing that the attack can be performed on client devices, and they have not released full-attack scripts to fully carry out the attacks against established networks. It should be noted, however, that they have announced that Android and Linux distributions are vulnerable to a key reinstall attack that forces the use of an all-zero key, effectively making traffic decryption trivial.

Time for action – getting KRACKing

We will now go through using the scripts as distributed through Mathy VanHoef's GitHub page.

1. First, open a terminal in Kali and type the command as shown in the following screenshot:

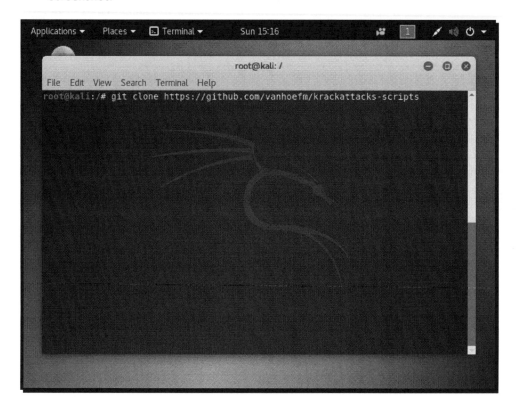

2. We will have to install the dependencies that the project relies upon. This will be achieved with the following command:

```
apt-get install libnl-3-dev libnl-genl-3-dev pkg-config libssl-dev
net-tools git sysfsutils python-scapy python-pycryptodome
```

3. Change into the created `krackattacks-scripts` directory and check the contents. It should look like the following:

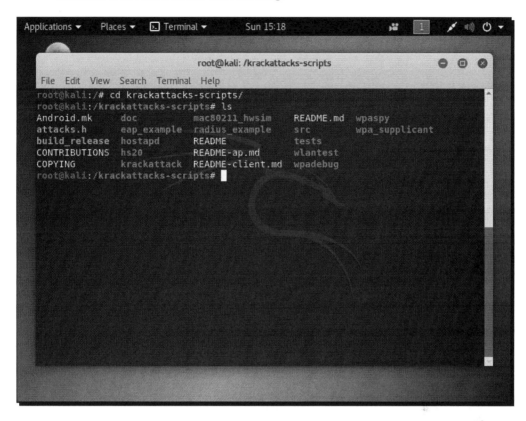

In this folder you can see the body of testing scripts and the solution Mathy and the team have put together. Before we can start playing with them, though, we need to compile `hostapd` in the format that they need.

The script itself provides these instructions on first use. However, I've written them here for clarity.

4. Change into the hostapd directory using the commands shown in the following screenshot:

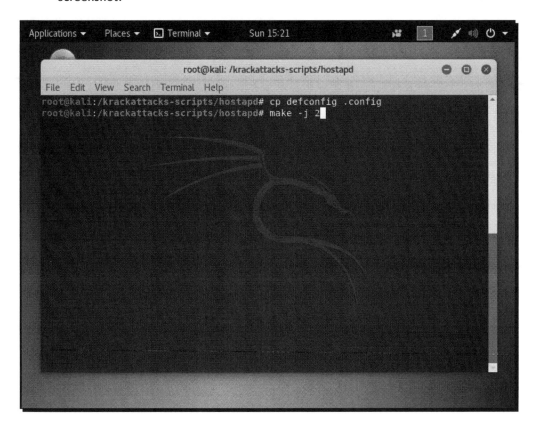

This will have compiled `hostapd` for use in the KRACK attack PoC scripts. To verify that it's built correctly, the folder should look like the following:

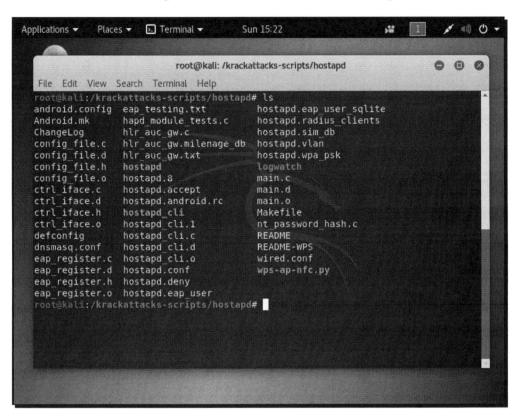

5. Change into the `krackattack` directory in the project root directory. It should look like the following screenshot:

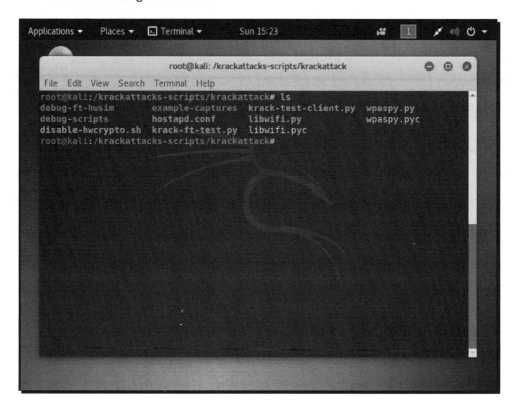

The scripts will recommend executing the `disable-hwcrypto.sh` script upon first use. However, after using an Alfa AWUS051NH and a Kali Linux VM, I found that this script would only crash the VM and the scripts worked regardless. It is a user's choice whether to carry this step out, but discretion is advised.

There are three other important files in this directory. Firstly, `hostapd.conf` defines the Wi-Fi details of the network to be generated. The defaults are `testnetwork` as the SSID and `abcdefgh` as the passphrase. Feel free to change these to your satisfaction.

Second, the `krack-test-client.py` script is the script that we will be using to identify vulnerable devices. This is the main focus of this chapter.

Finally, there is the `krack-ft-test.py` which we will not cover the usage of in this chapter due to its application to niche wireless devices outside of the standard distribution.

Next, we actually get *KRACKing*.

6. We will need to disable network manager to avoid conflicts using the following commands:

```
systemctl stop NetworkManager.service

systemctl disable NetworkManager.service
```

7. We can then execute the `krack-test-client.py` script with the following command:

```
python krack-test-client.py
```

You will then see the following screenshot:

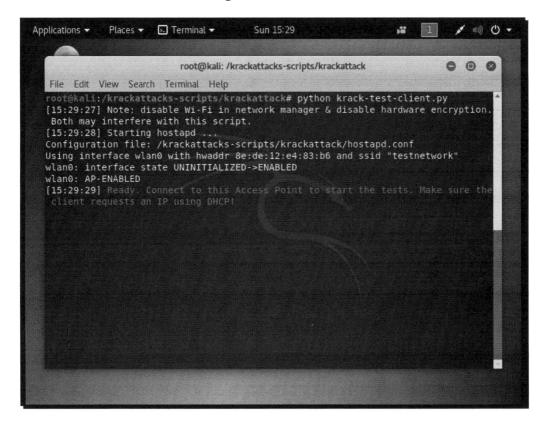

8. Now get hold of a test device, any Wi-Fi-enabled device, and connect to the created network with the credentials described earlier or whatever you've set it to.

The terminal will fill with text, but the script will helpfully mark any successful attacks in green as shown in the following screenshot:

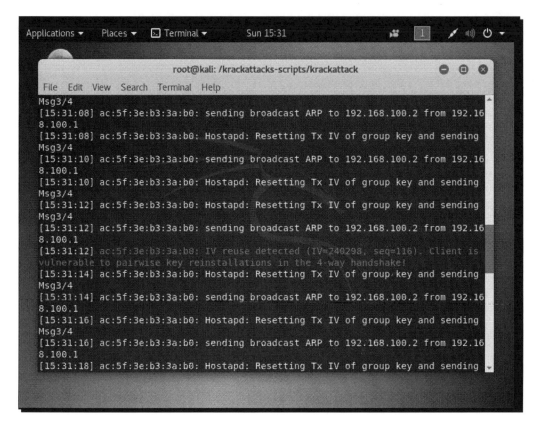

The script will iterate through the potential attacks and inform the user whether the device tested is vulnerable.

What just happened?

We successfully retrieved the PoC from Mathy VanHoef's GitHub page and tested a user device to see if it's vulnerable.

Summary

In this chapter, we've gone over the new KRACK attack, covered how the WPA2 handshake works, and saw how to perform a PoC check against a device. The KRACK attack will develop as time goes on and more scripts are released into the wild. Readers should keep up with the community and monitor for new and interesting applications of this research.

Readers should also visit the researcher's web page at `https://www.krackattacks.com/`.

Also, read the white paper for a greater understanding found at `https://papers.mathyvanhoef.com/ccs2017.pdf`.

9
Attacking WPA-Enterprise and RADIUS

"The bigger they are, the harder they Fall."

– Popular Saying

WPA-Enterprise has always had an aura of unbreakable ability around it. Most network administrators think of it as a panacea for all their wireless security problems. In this chapter, we will see that nothing could be further from the truth.

In this chapter, we will learn how to attack WPA-Enterprise using different tools and techniques available on Kali.

In this chapter, we will cover the following topics:

- Setting up FreeRADIUS-WPE
- Attacking PEAP on Windows clients
- Security best practices for enterprises

Setting up FreeRADIUS-WPE

We will need a RADIUS server for orchestrating WPA-Enterprise attacks. The most widely used open source RADIUS server is FreeRADIUS. However, setting it up is difficult and configuring it for each attack can be tedious.

Joshua Wright, a well-known security researcher, created a patch for FreeRADIUS that makes it easier to set up and conduct attacks. This patch was released as the FreeRADIUS-WPE (**Wireless Pwnage Edition**). Kali doesn't naturally come with FreeRADIUS-WPE, so you need to perform the following steps to set up FreeRADIUS-WPE:

Install FreeRADIUS-WPE with `apt-get install freeradius-wpe`. Now check your output to ensure it looks like the following screenshot:

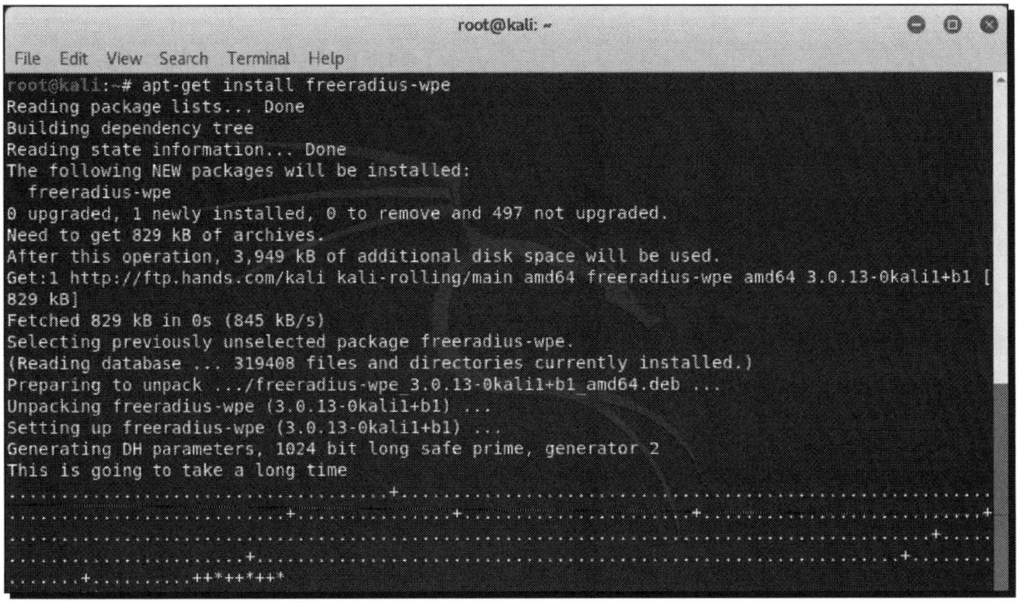

Let's now quickly set up the RADIUS server on Kali.

Time for action – setting up the AP with FreeRADIUS-WPE

Follow these instructions to get started:

1. Connect one of the LAN ports of the access point to the Ethernet port on your machine running Kali. In our case, the interface is `eth0`. Bring up the interface and get an IP address by running DHCP, as shown in the following screenshot:

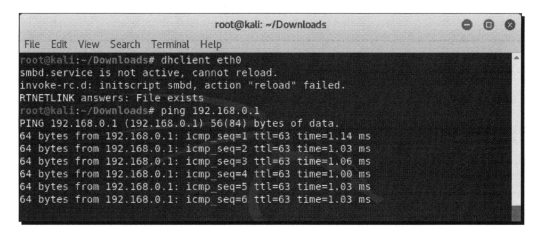

2. Log in to the access point and set the security mode to **WPA/WPA2-Enterprise**, set **Version** to **WPA2**, **Encryption** to **AES**. Then, under the EAP (802.1x) section, enter the **Radius Server IP** address as your Kali build's IP address. The **Radius Password** will be `test`, as shown in the following screenshot:

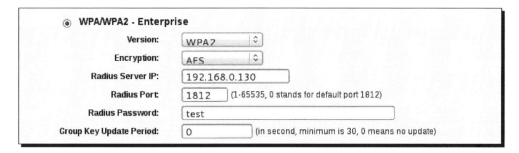

3. Let's now open a new terminal and go to the directory `/etc/freeradius-wpe/3.0`. This is where all the FreeRADIUS-WPE configuration files are.

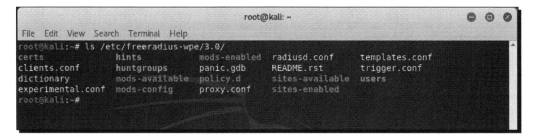

4. Let's open /mods-available/eap. You will find that the default_eap_type command is set to md5.

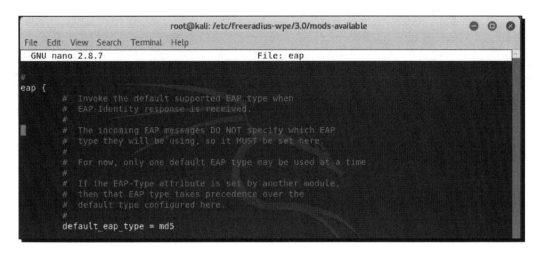

5. Let's change this to peap:

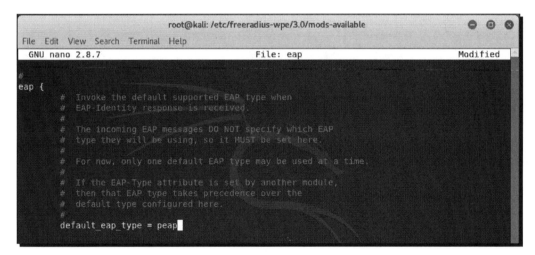

6. Let's open clients.conf. This is where we define the allowed list of clients that can connect to our RADIUS server. Interestingly, if you browse right to the bottom, ignoring the example settings, the secret for clients defaults to testing123. We want to change this to test to match step 2:

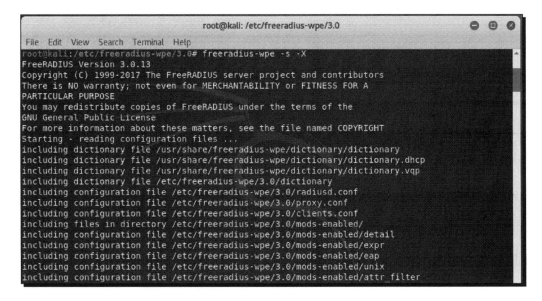

7. We are now all set to start the RADIUS server with the `freeradius-wpe -s -X` command:

8. Once you run this, you will see a lot of debug messages on the screen, but eventually the server will settle down to listen for requests. Awesome! We are all set now to start our lab sessions in this chapter.

What just happened?

We have successfully set up FreeRADIUS-WPE. We will use this in the rest of the experiments that we will do in this chapter.

Have a go hero – playing with RADIUS

FreeRADIUS-WPE has tons of options. It may be a good idea to familiarize yourself with them. Most importantly, take time to check out the different configuration files and how they all work together.

Attacking PEAP

Protected Extensible Authentication Protocol (PEAP) is the most popular version of EAP in use. This is the EAP mechanism shipped natively with Windows.

PEAP has two versions:

- ◆ PEAPv0 with EAP-MSCHAPv2 (the most popular as this has native support on Windows)
- ◆ PEAPv1 with EAP-GTC

PEAP uses server-side certificates for validation of the RADIUS server. Almost all attacks on PEAP leverage misconfigurations in certificate validation.

In the next lab, we will take a look at how to crack PEAP when certificate validation is turned off on the client.

Time for action – cracking PEAP

Follow the given instructions to get started:

 1. We double-check the `eap.conf` file to ensure that PEAP is enabled:

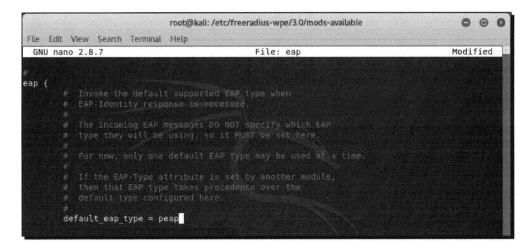

2. We then restart the RADIUS server with `freeradius-wpe -s -X`:

```
root@kali:/etc/freeradius-wpe/3.0# freeradius-wpe -s -X
FreeRADIUS Version 3.0.13
Copyright (C) 1999-2017 The FreeRADIUS server project and contributors
There is NO warranty; not even for MERCHANTABILITY or FITNESS FOR A
PARTICULAR PURPOSE
You may redistribute copies of FreeRADIUS under the terms of the
GNU General Public License
For more information about these matters, see the file named COPYRIGHT
Starting - reading configuration files ...
including dictionary file /usr/share/freeradius-wpe/dictionary/dictionary
including dictionary file /usr/share/freeradius-wpe/dictionary/dictionary.dhcp
including dictionary file /usr/share/freeradius-wpe/dictionary/dictionary.vqp
including dictionary file /etc/freeradius-wpe/3.0/dictionary
including configuration file /etc/freeradius-wpe/3.0/radiusd.conf
including configuration file /etc/freeradius-wpe/3.0/proxy.conf
including configuration file /etc/freeradius-wpe/3.0/clients.conf
including files in directory /etc/freeradius-wpe/3.0/mods-enabled/
including configuration file /etc/freeradius-wpe/3.0/mods-enabled/detail
including configuration file /etc/freeradius-wpe/3.0/mods-enabled/expr
including configuration file /etc/freeradius-wpe/3.0/mods-enabled/eap
including configuration file /etc/freeradius-wpe/3.0/mods-enabled/unix
including configuration file /etc/freeradius-wpe/3.0/mods-enabled/attr_filter
```

3. We monitor the log file created by FreeRADIUS-WPE:

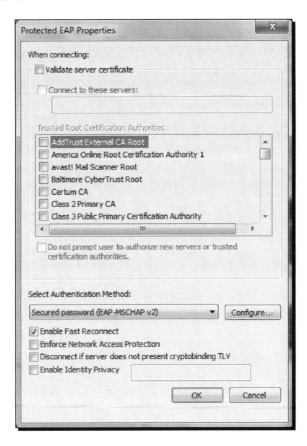


```
root@kali: /etc/freeradius-wpe/3.0
File  Edit  View  Search  Terminal  Help
root@kali:/etc/freeradius-wpe/3.0# tail -f /var/log/freeradius-wpe/radius.log
Sat Dec 16 13:28:45 2017 : Info: Debugger not attached
Sat Dec 16 13:28:45 2017 : Warning: [/etc/freeradius-wpe/3.0/mods-config/attr_filter/access_rej
ect]:11 Check item "FreeRADIUS-Response-Delay"  found in filter list for realm "DEFAULT".
Sat Dec 16 13:28:45 2017 : Warning: [/etc/freeradius-wpe/3.0/mods-config/attr_filter/access_rej
ect]:11 Check item "FreeRADIUS-Response-Delay-USec"      found in filter list for realm "DEFAULT
".
Sat Dec 16 13:28:45 2017 : Info: Loaded virtual server <default>
Sat Dec 16 13:28:45 2017 : Warning: Ignoring "sql" (see raddb/mods-available/README.rst)
Sat Dec 16 13:28:45 2017 : Warning: Ignoring "ldap" (see raddb/mods-available/README.rst)
Sat Dec 16 13:28:45 2017 : Info: # Skipping contents of 'if' as it is always 'false' -- /etc/f
reeradius-wpe/3.0/sites-enabled/inner-tunnel:330
Sat Dec 16 13:28:45 2017 : Info: Loaded virtual server inner-tunnel
Sat Dec 16 13:28:45 2017 : Info: Loaded virtual server default
Sat Dec 16 13:28:45 2017 : Info: Ready to process requests
```

4. Windows has native support for PEAP. Let's ensure that certificate verification has been turned off:

5. We need to click on the **Configure** tab that is next to **Secured password (EAP-MSCHAP v2)** and tell Windows not to automatically use our Windows logon name and password:

6. We will also have to force it to select **User authentication** in the **Advanced Settings** dialog box:

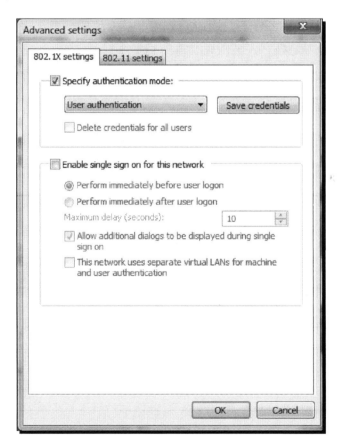

7. Once the client connects to the access point, the client is prompted for a username and password. We use `Monster` as the username and `abcdefghi` as the password:

8. As soon as we do this, you should be able to see the MSCHAP-v2 challenge response appear in the log file.

9. We now use `asleap` to crack this using a password list file that contains the password `abcdefghi`, and we are able to crack the password!

What just happened?

We set up our Honeypot using FreeRADIUS-WPE. The enterprise client is misconfigured to not use certificate validation with PEAP. This allows us to present our own fake certificate to the client, which it gladly accepts. Once this happens, MSCHAP-v2, the inner authentication protocol, kicks in. As the client uses our fake certificate to encrypt the data, we are easily able to recover the username, challenge, and response tuples.

MSCHAP-v2 is prone to dictionary attacks. We use `asleap` to crack the challenge and response pair, as it seems to be based on a dictionary word.

Have a go hero – attack variations on PEAP

PEAP can be misconfigured in multiple ways. Even with certificate validation enabled, if the administrator does not mention the authentic servers in connect to these servers list, the attacker can obtain a real certificate for another domain from any of the listed certifying authorities. This will still be accepted by the client. Other variations of this attack are possible as well.

We will encourage you to explore the different possibilities in this section.

EAP-TTLS

We encourage you to try attacks similar to those we have suggested for PEAP against EAP-TTLS.

Security best practices for enterprises

We have seen a ton of attacks against WPA/WPA2, both Personal and Enterprise. Based on our experience, we recommend the following:

- For SOHOs and medium-sized businesses, use WPA2-PSK with a strong passphrase. You have up to 63 characters at your disposal. Make use of them.

- For large enterprises, use WPA2-Enterprise with EAP-TLS. This uses both the client- and server-side certificates for authentication, and currently is unbreakable.

- If you have to use PEAP or EAP-TTLS with WPA2-Enterprise, then ensure that certificate validation is turned on, the right certifying authorities are chosen, RADIUS servers that are authorized are used, and finally, that any setting that allows users to accept new RADIUS servers, certificates, or certifying authorities is turned off.

Pop quiz – attacking WPA-Enterprise and RADIUS

Q1. Which of the following is FreeRADIUS-WPE?

1. A RADIUS server written from scratch
2. A patch to the FreeRADIUS server
3. Ships by default on all Linuxes
4. None of the above

Q2. Which of the following can be used to attack PEAP?

1. Fake credentials
2. Fake certificates
3. Using WPA-PSK
4. All of the above

Q3. What does EAP-TLS use?

1. Client-side certificates

2. Server-side certificates

3. Either 1 or 2

4. Both 1 and 2

Q4. What does EAP-TTLS use?

1. Client-side certificates only

2. Server-side certificates

3. Password-based authentication

4. LEAP

Summary

In this chapter, we saw how we could compromise the security of a WPA-Enterprise network running PEAP or EAP-TTLS, the two most common authentication mechanisms used in enterprises.

In the next chapter, we will take a look at how to put all that we have learned into use during an actual penetration test.

10
WLAN Penetration Testing Methodology

"The proof is in the pudding."

— Popular saying

This chapter will lay out the steps that go in to taking the techniques taught in the previous chapters and turning them into a full wireless penetration test.

Wireless penetration testing

To perform a wireless penetration test, it is important to follow a defined methodology. Simply firing up the `airbase` or `airodump` command and hoping for the best will not satisfy the goals of a test. When working as a penetration tester, you must ensure that you adhere to the standards of the organization you're working for, and if they don't have any, then you should hold yourself to the highest standards.

Broadly, we can break up a wireless penetration testing exercise into the following phases:

1. Planning phase
2. Discovery phase
3. Attack phase
4. Reporting phase

We will now look at each of these phases separately.

Planning

In this phase, we must understand the following:

- **Scope of the assessment**: The penetration tester should work with the client to define a scope that is achievable and will also provide the greatest amount of insight into the security of a network. Typically, the following information is gathered:

  - Location of the penetration test.
  - Total coverage area of the premises.
  - Approximate number of access points and wireless clients deployed.
  - Which wireless networks are included in the assessment?
  - Is exploitation in scope?
  - Are attacks against users in scope?
  - Is denial of service in scope?

- **Effort estimation**: Based on the scope defined, the tester will then have to estimate how much time is required. Bear in mind that rescoping may occur following this estimate, as organizations may have limited resources available in terms of both time and money.

- **Legality**: Prior to performing a test, the client must give consent. This should explain the testing to be covered and clearly define the level of indemnity, insurance, and the limitations of the scope. If you are unsure, you will need to speak to a professional in these areas. Most organizations will have their own versions that will likely also incorporate a **Non-Disclosure Agreement (NDA)**.

Once all of the preceding requirements are in place, we are ready to go!

Discovery

In this phase, the aim is to identify and apply characteristics to the wireless devices and wireless networks within the scope.

All the techniques to perform these have been laid out in the previous chapters but, in brief, the aim is to:

- Enumerate visible and hidden wireless networks in the area
- Enumerate devices in the area, along with those connected to the targeted networks
- Map the range of the networks, where they are reachable from and whether there are places a malicious individual could operate from to perform an attack, for example, a cafe

All of this information should be recorded. If the test is limited to the performance of reconnaissance only, the test will end here, and the tester will attempt to draw conclusions based on this information. Some statements that would be useful to a client are as follows:

- The number of devices that have associations with open networks and the corporate network
- The number of devices that have networks that can be linked to locations through solutions such as WiGLE
- The existence of weak encryption
- The networks are too restrictive and block standard users

Attack

Once reconnaissance has been performed, exploitation must be performed for proof of concept. If the attack is being performed as part of a red team or wider assessment, then exploitation should be performed to gain access to the network as surreptitiously as possible.

In our attacking phase, we will explore the following:

- Cracking the encryption
- Attacking the infrastructure
- Compromising clients
- Finding vulnerable clients
- Finding unauthorized clients

Cracking the encryption

The first step is to retrieve the keys for any vulnerable networks identified. If networks with WEP exist, perform the WEP-cracking methods explained in *Chapter 4, WLAN Encryption Flaws*. Regardless of whether you can crack it or not though, the presence of WEP is still considered a vulnerability. If WPA2-secured systems are present, you have two choices. If aiming to be stealthy, arrive on-site at times when individuals are likely to be authenticating or re-authenticating. These times are likely to be:

- Start of the day
- Lunch time
- End of the day

At this time, set up your WPA key retrieval setup as shown in *Chapter 4, WLAN Encryption Flaws*. Alternatively, perform the deauthentication attack, as shown in *Chapter 6, Attacking the Client*.

This is noisier and more likely to be detected in a mature organization.

If WPA-Enterprise is in place, bear in mind you will have to use the information gathered from the reconnaissance to target the correct network and set up your dummy Enterprise setup as shown in the *Attacking PEAP* section in *Chapter 9, Attacking WPA-Enterprise and RADIUS*.

You can attempt to break all passphrases but bear in mind that some will be unbreakable. Following the performance of the test, check with the wireless administrator for the passphrase in use. Check to see whether it is a secure passphrase and that you, as a tester, did not experience a tool failure or were merely unlucky.

Attacking infrastructure

If network access is gained through cracking the encryption, perform a standard network penetration test if allowed in scope. The following should be performed as a minimum:

- A port scan
- Identifying which services are running
- Enumerating any open services, such as unauthenticated FTP, SMB, or HTTP
- Exploiting any vulnerable services identified

Compromising clients

After enumerating and testing all wireless systems, there are various types of engagements that would suit performing attacks against clients.

If necessary, after establishing which clients are vulnerable to KARMA attacks, create a Honeypot to force them to connect with the methods laid out in the *Attacking PEAP* section in *Chapter 9, Attacking WPA-Enterprise and RADIUS*. There are various useful pieces of information that can be gathered through this method, but ensure that the collected data serves a purpose and is stored, transmitted, and used in an ethical and safe manner.

Reporting

Finally, at the end of testing, it is necessary to report your findings to the client. It's important to ensure that the report matches the quality of your testing. As the client will only see the report, you have to give it as much love and attention as you do to your testing. The following is a guideline to the layout of the report:

1. Management summary
2. Technical summary
3. Findings:
   - Vulnerability description
   - Severity
   - Affected devices
   - Vulnerability type—software/hardware/configuration
   - Remediation
4. Appendices

The **management summary** should be aimed at talking to a senior nontechnical audience with a focus on the effects and mitigations required at a high level. Avoid language that is too technical and ensure that the root causes are covered.

The **technical summary** should be a midpoint between the management summary and findings list. It should be aimed at a developer or a technical lead with a focus on how to fix the issues and broad solutions that could be implemented.

The findings list should describe each vulnerability at a low level, explaining the methods to identify, and replicate, and vulnerabilities.

Appendices should contain any extra information that would be too long to describe in a short description. This is where any screenshots, proof-of-concept code, or stolen data should be presented.

Summary

In this chapter, we discussed a methodology for performing a range of wireless tests and referred to the relevant chapters for each step. We also listed methods for reporting vulnerabilities and techniques for making technical data presentable. In the next and final chapter, we will cover new techniques developed since the initial publication of this book, WPS, and probe monitoring for surveillance.

11
WPS and Probes

"Nothing is new under the sun."

– Popular Saying

This chapter incorporates the new techniques related to attacking WPS and probe monitoring and also covers the pineapple tool that makes much of wireless testing a lot easier. These attacks and tools have appeared since the publication of the original book, and we'll be making sure we're being as holistic as possible.

WPS attacks

Wireless Protected Setup (WPS) was introduced in 2006 to help users without wireless knowledge to have secure networks. The idea was that their Wi-Fi device would have a single hidden hardcoded value that would allow access with key memorization. New devices would be authenticated through a button press on the Wi-Fi router. Individuals outside the house without access to the device would not be able to have access, thus reducing the issues surrounding remembering WPA keys or setting short ones.

In late 2011, a security vulnerability was disclosed enabling brute-force attacks on the WPS authentication system. The traffic required to negotiate a WPS exchange was spoofable, and the WPS pin itself is only eight characters between 0-9. To start with, this provides only 100,000,000 possibilities in comparison with an eight-character azAZ09 password having 218,340,105,584,896 combinations.

However, there are further vulnerabilities:

◆ Of the eight characters of the WPS pin, the last character is a checksum of the previous seven and therefore predictable, leaving a maximum of 10,000,000 options

◆ In addition, the first four and the following three of the remaining characters are checked separately, which means that there are $10^4 + 10^3$ options or 11,000

Through the two decisions made in the authentication mechanism, we have gone from 100,000,000 possible combinations to 11,000. This equates to a six-hour difference when brute-forcing the algorithm. It is these decisions that make attacks against WPS viable.

In the next lab exercise, we will go through identifying and attacking vulnerable WPS setups with Wash and Reaver.

Time for action – WPS attack

Follow the given instructions to get started:

1. Before we attack a WPS-enabled access point, we need to create one. The TP-Link we use has this feature turned on by default, which is worrying but handy. To double-check this, we can log onto our router and click on **WPS**. It should look like the following:

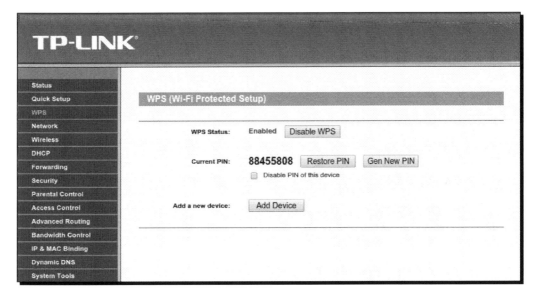

2. Now we've confirmed that it's ready. We need to set up our target. We need to set up our testing environment. We're going to use the Wash tool, and Wash requires a monitoring interface to function. As we have done many times before, we need to set up one with the following command:

```
airmon-ng start wlan0
```

The output will be as follows:

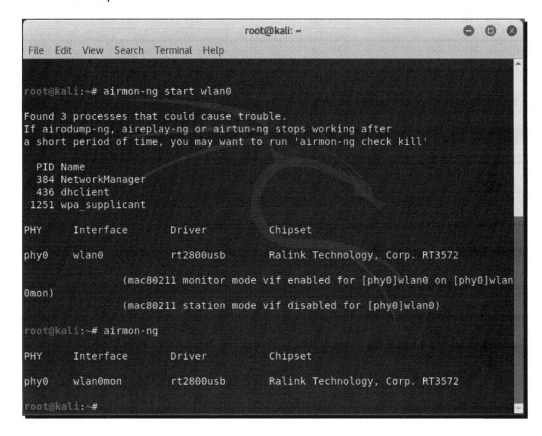

3. We have a monitoring interface set up as `wlan0mon`, and we can call Wash with the following command:

```
wash -i wlan0mon
```

4. Wash will display all the nearby devices that support WPS as well as whether they have WPS active or unlocked and what version is running:

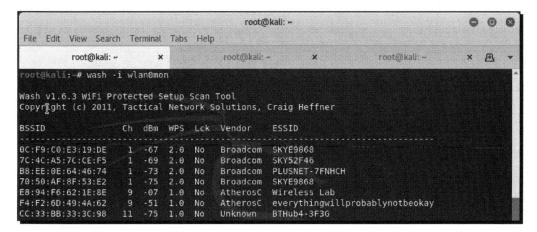

5. We can see the `Wireless Lab` network supports WPS. It uses version 1 and it's not locked. Fantastic. We take note of the MAC address, which in my case is `E8:94:F6:62:1E:8E`, as this will be used to target our next tool: `reaver`.

6. Reaver attempts to brute-force the WPS pin for a given MAC address. The syntax for starting this is as follows:

```
reaver -i wlan0mon -b <mac> -vv
```

The output will be as follows:

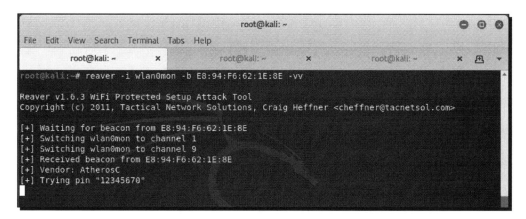

7. Once it is started, the tool runs through all the possible combinations for the WPS and attempts to authenticate. Once it does this, it will return the WPS code and the password, as shown in the following screenshot:

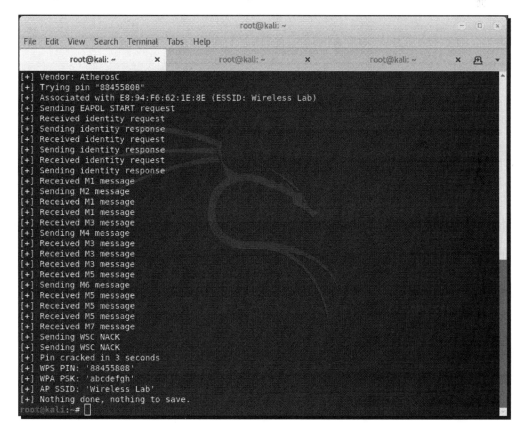

8. With WPA-PSK in hand, we can authenticate normally now. I left my device with the default WPA-PSK that matches the WPS pin. If, however, you want to authenticate with the WPS pin, you can do this by specifying the pin in `reaver` with the following command:

```
reaver -i wlan0mon -b <mac> -vv -p 88404148
```

Replace my pin with your own.

What just happened?

We successfully identified a wireless network with a vulnerable instance of WPS active with Wash. We then used Reaver to recover the WPA key and the WPS pin. With this information, we could then authenticate with the network and continue a network penetration test.

Have a go hero – rate limiting

In the previous exercise, we attacked an entirely unprotected WPS installation. There are multiple methods that can be used to further secure installations without removing WPS altogether.

Make an attempt to set the WPS pin to an arbitrary value and try again, to see whether Reaver is as effective at cracking it.

Acquire a wireless router that allows you to rate-limit the WPS attempts. Try and configure your attack to avoid triggering lockouts.

Probe sniffing

We have spoken about probes previously, and how they can be used to identify hidden networks and perform effective rogue access point attacks. They can also be used to identify individuals as targets or track them on a mass scale with minimal equipment.

When a device wishes to connect to a network, it sends a probe request that contains its own MAC address and the name of the network it wishes to connect to. We can use tools such as `airodump-ng` to track these. However, if we wish to identify whether an individual was present at a specific location at a specific time or look for trends in Wi-Fi usage, we will need to use a different approach.

In this section, we will utilize `tshark` and Python to collect data. You will receive the code and an explanation of what is being done.

Time for action – collecting data

Follow the given instructions to get started:

1. First of all, we need a device that's looking for multiple networks. Generally, a normal smartphone such as an Android device or iPhone will do the trick. Desktops don't generally make good targets as they tend to remain in one location. Newer iPhones and Android devices may have probe requests disabled or obfuscated, so do check before you give up.

2. Once you have your device, make sure the Wi-Fi is turned on.

3. Then set up your monitoring interface as we have done many times before:

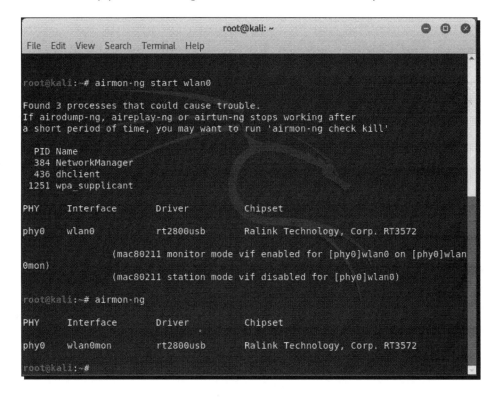

```
root@kali:~# airmon-ng start wlan0

Found 3 processes that could cause trouble.
If airodump-ng, aireplay-ng or airtun-ng stops working after
a short period of time, you may want to run 'airmon-ng check kill'

  PID Name
  384 NetworkManager
  436 dhclient
 1251 wpa_supplicant

PHY     Interface        Driver           Chipset

phy0    wlan0            rt2800usb        Ralink Technology, Corp. RT3572

            (mac80211 monitor mode vif enabled for [phy0]wlan0 on [phy0]wlan
0mon)
            (mac80211 station mode vif disabled for [phy0]wlan0)

root@kali:~# airmon-ng

PHY     Interface        Driver           Chipset

phy0    wlan0mon         rt2800usb        Ralink Technology, Corp. RT3572

root@kali:~#
```

4. The next thing to be done is to look for probe requests with tshark via the following command:

```
tshark -n -i wlan0mon subtype probereq
```

The screenshot of the following command is as follows:

5. Your output at this point is a little rough, as the default output from `tshark` is not designed to be readable, just to have as much information in it as possible. It should look like the following:

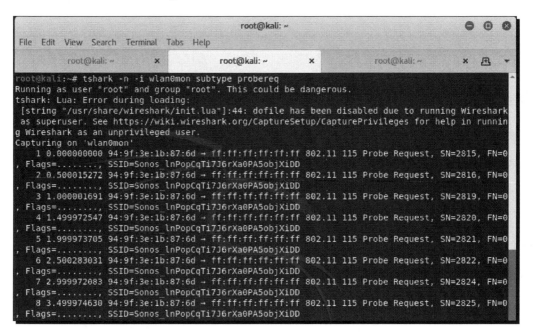

6. You can clearly see the MAC address and SSID of the probe request; however, this output can be improved. We can use the following command to make it more readable:

```
tshark -n -i wlan0mon -T fields -e wlan.sa -e wlan.ssid
```

The screenshot of the following command is as follows:

7. The output here is much more readable:

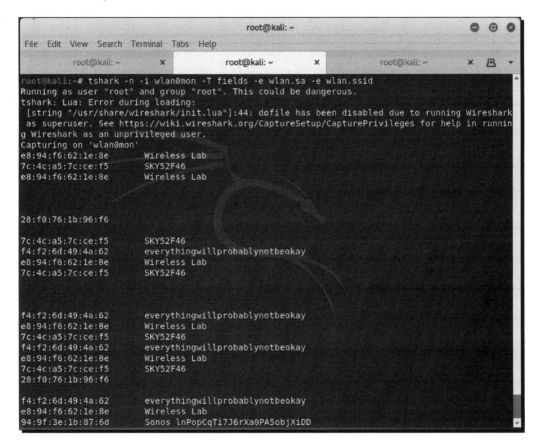

8. So, now we have the output in a readable format, what next? What we do is create a Python script that will run the command and record the output for later analysis. Before running the code, you will need to ensure that you have your monitoring interface ready and that a file called `results.txt` is created in the directory you are in. The Python script is as follows:

```python
import subprocess
import datetime
results = open("results.txt", "a")
while 1:
    cmd = subprocess.check_output(["tshark -n -i wlan0mon -T
fields -e wlan.sa -e wlan.ssid -c 100"], shell=True)
    split = cmd.split("\n")
    for value in split[:-1]:
            if value.strip():
                    splitvalue = value.split("\t")
                    MAC = str(splitvalue[0])
                    SSID = str(splitvalue[1])
                    time = str(datetime.datetime.now())
                    results.write(MAC+" "+SSID+" "+time+"\r\n")
```

Let's get briefed on the Python script:

- ❏ `import subprocess` and `import datetime`: This allow us to refer to the `subprocess` and `datetime` libraries. The `subprocess` library allows us to monitor the interface from the Linux command line, and `datetime` allows us to get the accurate time and date readings.

- ❏ `results = open("results.txt", "a")`: This opens a file with the append rights and assigns it to `results`. The append rights only allow the script to add to the contents of the file. This stops the file from constantly being overwritten.

- ❏ `while 1`: This line means run until stopped.

- ❏ `cmd = subprocess.check_output(["tshark -n -i wlan0mon -T fields -e wlan.sa -e wlan.ssid -c 100"], shell=True)`: This opens a shell to perform our previously tested `tshark` command. The only difference this time is `-c 100`. What this flag does is limit the command to 100 queries. This allows us to return the results to ourselves without having to stop the program. Since we said run forever after writing the results, the script will restart again. This line takes the output from the shell and assigns it to the variable `cmd`. The script will display a count to 100, stop, and then restart. This means that if you want it to end, you have to kill the process.

- ❏ `split = cmd.split("\n")`: This takes the variable and splits it by line.
- ❏ `for value in split[:-1]`: This repeats the following action for each line in the output, ignoring the first line that contains headers.
- ❏ `if value.strip()`: This checks to see if the value is empty before continuing to account for non-probe requests.
- ❏ `value = value.split("\t")`: This breaks each line into further smaller chunks using the tab character as the delimiter.
- ❏ The following three lines take each chunk of text and assign it to a variable:
  ```
  MAC = str(splitvalue[0])
  SSID = str(splitvalue[1])
  time = str(datetime.datetime.now())
  ```
- ❏ `results.write(MAC+" "+SSID+" "+time+"\r\n")`: This takes all the values, writes them to a file separated by spaces, and ends with a return and a new line for neatness. The output will be neat lines of text written to the file.

What just happened?

We took the input from probe requests and output them to a file using Python. You may ask yourself what the purpose of this is. This can be achieved by simply performing the original `tshark` command and adding a `>> results.txt` command to the end. You would be correct; however, what we have created is a framework for integration with other tools, visualization platforms, databases, and services.

For example, using the WiGLE database that maps SSIDs to locations, you can add a few lines of code to take the SSID variable and query the WiGLE database. Alternatively, you could set up a MySQL database and output the results there to perform the SQL commands on it. This section has provided you with the first steps to create your own probe-monitoring tools. Through experimentation and using this simple code as the first step, a multitude of useful tools can be created.

Have a go hero – extension ideas

Research which tools are available that allow visualization or data analytics and are easily integrated with Python. Tools such as Maltego have free versions that can be used to plot information.

Set yourself up a MySQL database to record the data and reconfigure the preceding Python script to output the results to the database. Then, build another script (or do it in the same one) to retrieve the data and output it to Maltego.

Reconfigure the script to query WiGLE, and collect geolocation data for probe requests. Output this data through Maltego.

Make an attempt to set up a web-based frontend through Flask, Django, or PHP to display your results. Investigate currently existing solutions for presenting the data and attempting to emulate or improve them through a discussion with their creators.

Summary

In this chapter, we discussed the attacks against WPS that have come about since the release of the original book and also performed an initial foray into integrating wireless tools with Python. Alas, we have come to end of the book, I hope it's been informative and interesting.

Pop Quiz Answers

Chapter 1, Wireless Lab Setup

Pop quiz – understanding the basics

Q1	Run the command ifconfig wlan0. In the output, you should see a flag "UP", this indicates that the card is functional.
Q2	You will only need a hard drive if you would like to store anything across reboots like configuration settings or scripts.
Q3	It shows the ARP table on the local machine.
Q4	We would use WPA_Supplicant.

Chapter 2, WLAN and Its Inherent Insecurities

Pop quiz – understanding the basics

Q1	3
Q2	3
Q3	1

Chapter 3, Bypassing WLAN Authentication

Pop quiz – WLAN authentication

Q1	4
Q2	2
Q3	1

Chapter 4, WLAN Encryption Flaws

Pop quiz – WLAN encryption flaws

Q1	3
Q2	1

Chapter 5, Attacks on the WLAN Infrastructure

Pop quiz – attacks on the WLAN infrastructure

Q1	1
Q2	1
Q3	1
Q3	4

Chapter 6, Attacking the Client

Pop quiz – Attacking the Client

Q1	1
Q2	1
Q3	2
Q3	4

Chapter 7, Advanced WLAN Attacks

Pop quiz – advanced WLAN attacks

Q1	2
Q2	2
Q3	4
Q3	1

Chapter 9, Attacking WPA-Enterprise and RADIUS

Pop quiz – attacking WPA-Enterprise and RADIUS

Q1	2
Q2	2
Q3	4
Q3	2

Index

82659581R00117

Made in the USA
Middletown, DE
04 August 2018